JOHN MARSTON

The Malcontent

with a Commentary by
SIMON TRUSSLER

and Notes by
WILLIAM NAISMITH

A Methuen Paperback

Methuen Student Editions: London and New York

This Methuen Student Edition first published in 1987
by Methuen London Ltd, 11 New Fetter Lane, London EC4P 4EE
and Methuen Inc., 29 West 35th Street, New York NY 10001

British Library Cataloguing in Publication Data

Marston, John, 1575-1634
 The malcontent. — (Methuen student
 editions).
 I. Title   II. Trussler, Simon
 III. Naismith, William
 822'.3   PR2694.M3

 ISBN 0-413-16290-7

*Thanks are due to Tricia Hern for help
in the preparation of this edition.*

Set by 🖪 Tek Art Ltd., Croydon, Surrey
Printed and bound in Great Britain
by Richard Clay Ltd
Bungay, Suffolk

Contents

CONTENTS

John Marston: 1576–1634

1576 Born, presumably near Wardington, in Oxfordshire, where he was christened on 7 October, son of a Middle Temple lawyer from an old Shropshire family, also John Marston, and of Maria Guarsi, daughter of a wealthy Italian surgeon. Probably brought up in Coventry.

1591 Took up residence at Brasenose College, Oxford, but did not matriculate until 4 February 1592.

1592 2 August, admitted to study law in the Middle Temple.

1594 23 March, graduated with B.A. Degree from Oxford.

1595 November, known to be residing in London, and to be sharing his father's chambers in the Middle Temple from June 1597.

1598 Pseudonymous publication of his collection of satirical and erotic verse, *The Metamorphosis of Pygmalion's Image, and Certain Satires,* and of a second collection of verse satires, *The Scourge of Villainy,* revised in 1599.

1599 Came into his inheritance (presumably considerable) on the death of his father, and subsequently of independent means. 1 June, Archbishop Whitgift of Canterbury and Bishop Bancroft of London ordered the destruction by burning of satirical writings, including both Marston's collections. 28 Sept., accounts of the theatrical manager Henslowe record payment to him for share in revision of a lost play, *Robert II, King of Scots.* Also revised old play, *Histriomastix; or, The Player Whipped,* probably for a Middle Temple audience, and wrote the satirical romance *Antonio and Mellida,* among the first of the plays performed by the revived Children of Paul's company. Continued to write for these boy players for the next three years.

1600 *Antonio's Revenge,* sequel to *Antonio and Mellida,* performed by Children of Paul's — prompting Ben Jonson to satirize Marston for his 'fustian' (bombastic writing) in *Every Man out of His Humour,* which initiated the so-called 'war of the theatres'. Marston retaliated with the domestic satire *Jack Drum's Entertainment* for Paul's, portraying Jonson as the cuckold Brabant Senior.

1601 Contributed with Shakespeare, Chapman, and Jonson to *Love's Martyr,* honouring the recent knighthood of Sir John Salusbury of the Middle Temple — but expelled from his own chambers there on 14 Oct. for non-payment of dues and non-residence, possibly owing to the continuing 'war' in which Marston was further lampooned by Jonson in *The Poetaster* as the posturing poet Crispinus.

1602 Wrote the uncharacteristically romantic comedy *What You Will* for Paul's.

1603 End of the quarrel with Jonson marked by Marston's contribution of commendatory verses to Jonson's tragedy *Sejanus,* and later by the dedication to him of the published text of *The Malcontent,* the first version of which was probably performed in this year by the Children of the Chapel Royal.

1604 Revised *The Malcontent* for adult performance by the King's Men. Around this time, acquired a one-sixth share in the syndicate controlling the Children of the Chapel Royal, now under royal patronage as the Queen's Revels, performing at the Blackfriars. For them he now wrote the satirical *Parasitaster; or, The Fawn,* the earthy city comedy *The Dutch Courtesan,* and all his later plays.

1605 Married Mary Wilkes, daughter of a Wiltshire rector, with whom the couple probably lived till 1616. Collaborated with Chapman and Jonson on the mock city comedy *Eastward Ho!* and may have been imprisoned with them for satirical references to King James's Scottish nationality and sale of honours. Freed by November.

1606 Wrote the stoical tragedy *Sophonisba; or, The Wonder of Women,* and a civic pageant in Latin to celebrate the visit to London of King Christian of Denmark.

1607 Aug., his *Entertainment at Ashby* in honour of Alice, Dowager Countess of Derby, performed at Ashby-de-la-Zouche.

1608 8 June, committed by the Privy Council to Newgate, for an unknown reason — but possibly connected with his theatrical activities, since on his release he sold his share in the Queen's Revels, and wrote no further plays. *The Insatiate Countess,* left unfinished, thought to have been completed by William Barksted in 1613.

1609   24 Sept., ordained deacon in parish church of Stanton Harcourt, Oxfordshire, and (after becoming student at St. Mary Hall) ordained priest, 29 Dec.

1616   Presented with the curacy of Christchurch, Hampshire.

1621   Death of his mother, leaving him property in Coventry.

1624   Death in infancy of his only son, John.

1631   16 Sept., resigned the living at Christchurch.

1633   Objected to unauthorized publication of a collection of his plays, which was then reissued anonymously.

1634   25 June, died in London at 'Aldermanbury his house there', and buried beside his father in the Temple church.

Background to the play

The theatrical context

The Malcontent offers us perhaps the richest evidence available
from any single play of its time concerning the different staging
conditions of the two kinds of Elizabethan playhouse — for it is
unusual not only in having been performed in both a 'private' and
a 'public' theatre, but also in having been printed in successive
versions which reflect the change of venue. First seen in an indoor
playhouse, the second Blackfriars, sometime between 1600 and
early 1604, the play was then revised (and the Induction by John
Webster added) for performance outdoors at the Globe later in
1604.

'Private' theatres such as the Blackfriars were so called because
of the social exclusiveness of their smaller audiences, which had to
pay considerably higher prices for their protection from the
vagaries of the English climate. There was seating throughout such
theatres, in the rows of benches facing the stage as well as in the
galleries which flanked the auditorium on three sides — whereas at
'public' theatres such as the Globe most members of the audience
stood in the uncovered courtyard which surrounded a raised thrust
stage on three sides, and here the surrounding galleries, offering
both seats and some protection from the weather, were the more
expensive parts of the house.

Both kinds of theatre had first emerged in 1576, a few years
after the act which gave some security to those bands of actors able
to secure noble patronage, but they had developed to serve the
needs not only of different kinds of audiences but of different
kinds of actors. The public theatres were the preserve of the
companies of adult male actors, while the private playhouses came
to be occupied by the boy players, who were back in fashion at the
turn of the century after a decade in oblivion. This distinction had
become less important by 1609, when the children's companies
were once more out of favour, and the occupants of the Globe —
Shakespeare's company, the King's Men — took over the Blackfriars
as their winter home. Soon, such plays as Webster's *The Duchess of
Malfi* (c. 1613) could apparently be transferred without difficulty

from one kind of theatre to the other, according to the time of year: but only a little earlier, the 'private' and 'public' playhouses were also being served by rather different kinds of play — in part because of the physical differences in staging, but also because of the physical *and* psychological differences between companies of grown men and pre-pubescent choristers.

However precociously skilled (or simply precocious) the boy players became, they lacked the emotional maturity required for such complex roles as Shakespeare was creating for his company at the Globe. The playwrights attached to the children's companies, as was Marston for most of his theatrical career, therefore had to find ways in which the boys could exploit their apparent disadvantages — and there was, evidently, a ready audience of 'sophisticates' for plays in which small boys bawdily mimicked the sexual and social ways of their elders. But the resultant 'presentational' acting, which must have involved a mutual self-awareness between actors and audience, was also an excellent stylistic framework for satire — while in *The Malcontent*, Marston blended social satire and a strain of obsessive sexuality into a pattern made even more complex by the play's 'augmentation' for adult performance.

The original audiences of *The Malcontent* would also have had in their minds the recent 'war of the theatres', in which Marston and Ben Jonson had been leading antagonists, and which involved the renewed rivalries between the adult and boy players. The 'theatrical context' of this play is thus of more than merely historical interest, and will demand further discussion throughout this commentary; for the interaction here between theatrical conventions and what is being 'said' is more than usually close — and is even reflected in the title. The 'malcontent' is thus not only a 'character', but a theatrical type without some knowledge of which it is difficult fully to comprehend *Hamlet* — a product of these same years around the beginning of the new century, when the theatre more than any other art reflected a prevalent sense of malaise in men's attitude to their society.

From Elizabethan to Jacobean

The year which probably saw the production of *The Malcontent* in its first version, 1603, saw also the death of Queen Elizabeth and the succession of James I (and so, from the Latin form of the King's name, Jacobus, the beginning of the Jacobean age). Of course it is always dangerous to talk, especially at this distance in time, of such an event marking 'a change in the mood of the nation' – not least because our evidence can only be drawn from a relatively small literate elite. Especially for the less fortunate, there had been cause enough for unease in the last decade or so of the old Queen's reign, with rampant inflation, some disastrous harvests, and the Poor Laws now giving statutory recognition to the breakdown of a socially interdependent society. But the sheer, stubborn survival of the old Queen and the afterglow of final ascendancy at sea over Spain lent a deceptive sense of stability to Elizabeth's dying years, which in drama and literature saw the last flowering of late-renaissance confidence – alike in the aspirations of Marlovian heroes and the quiet pride in nation and selfhood displayed, say, by Dekker's Simon Eyre in *The Shoemakers' Holiday*. Dekker's career, of course, continued into the new reign, and in his pamphlet *The Wonderful Year 1603* he wrote of 'the general terror' bred by Elizabeth's death in the spring – which also brought with it another visitation of the plague.

We find the shifting mood reflected even in the works of that supposedly most 'universal' of writers, William Shakespeare. After the great romantic comedies of his maturity, the turn of the century saw him turning to those works which express the feeling of their times in the very label of 'problem plays' that modern critics have attached to them. These included *Measure for Measure,* with its own disguised Duke putting all to rights in a disordered court, and *Troilus and Cressida,* with its sour view of the way in which sexuality goes hand in hand with political ambition – often expressed through the railing Thersites, a malcontent whom some believe to have been modelled on Marston himself. And first in line of the great tragedies on which Shakespeare was now to embark came *Hamlet,* whose central character at once embodies and transcends any such typology.

By the late fifteen nineties, a new satirical edge was being honed in verse, and was soon to find a necessarily alternative medium in theatre. The Inns of Court, in whose intellectual society Marston now found himself, were a natural centre for the fashion in epigram and paradox which characterized the shift from the consciously balanced style of the Elizabethans to the asymmetric, 'metaphysical' concerns of the early Jacobeans. The questionable tastes and behaviour of the new monarch himself, the prevalence not only of the plague but of the more insidiously epidemic venereal disease, and an increasing awareness that the values of emergent capitalism were no aberration but marks of the final breakdown of belief in intrinsic value and 'nobless oblige' — all these disparate elements were not only the concerns of the new writers, but the forces which shaped their everyday lives.

We should, then, avoid the temptation to treat the 'golden age of English drama' (from roughly 1590 to even more roughly 1615) as a sort of organic whole — and we should also be aware of the special characteristics and interest of those works which, like *Hamlet* and *The Malcontent,* mark a sort of 'cusp' between the Elizabethan and Jacobean ages. None of the characters of our play has reached the stage of existential self-awareness of, say, Webster's Flamineo in *The White Devil* or Tourneur's Vindice in *The Revenger's Tragedy:* but they have lost that overweening confidence in their own ambitions which marked such late-renaissance dramatic heroes as Marlowe's Tamburlaine or Faustus. They may move in a mythical version of Genoa, but the concerns and uncertainties they express bring them very much closer to the London that was Marston's home.

Influences on Marston's thought

The Elizabethans were much less concerned than we are today with 'originality' in a work of drama or literature. Most writers kept a 'commonplace book' in which to jot down memorable lines from their reading or playgoing, and classical or modern quotations were often employed as *sententiae* — those pithy moral conclusions with which many playwrights bespattered their dialogue (and which are indicated in our text by italic type, or by opened quotation marks). Some writers, Webster notable among them, were able to transmute other men's thoughts almost alchemically into their own: others, such as Marston, were content to use more or less direct quotation as rhetorical punctuation-marks in their work. But, to suggest, as have some critics, that Marston's plays amount to little more than a ragbag of borrowings is to misunderstand the nature of the Elizabethan creative process — as also the quality of its reception by its original audience. Thus, although his early *Antonio* plays utilize elements from *The Spanish Tragedy* to *Hamlet,* these work as points of common reference for the self-aware coterie audiences of the Blackfriars. It is, of course, a limitation that few can hope to respond so knowledgeably (or knowingly) today, and *The Malcontent* is more accessible for us than Marston's earlier work precisely because its 'borrowings' and 'influences' have to do less with direct quotation, and more with ideas, conventions, and even character-types.

Although the play moves partly within the 'revenge tradition' (see further p. xxxv, below), the tensions which underlie it can be traced even further back, to the basic but irreconcilable components of the Elizabethan educational system — on the one hand, the philosophy and attitudes of mind derived from schooldays devoted to the Latin language and its 'pagan' authors, on the other the Christian thinking received through no less regular a diet of sermons and theological debate. Thus, while few writers of the period tried to fit their work into the rigid neoclassical straitjacket of the serious Italian (and later French) drama, many looked for guidance to the first-century Roman playwright Seneca — not so much for dramatic raw material, but because as a philosopher his stoic approach (of indifference to pleasure or pain) was reconcilable with the more ascetic forms of Christianity.

The struggle between the stoic absolutes of passion and reason thus found early theatrical expression in such blood-and-guts dramas as Kyd's *The Spanish Tragedy* and Shakespeare's *Titus Andronicus* — and later, at a more 'dignified' level, in Jonson's two tragedies, *Sejanus* and *Catiline*. And the stoical belief in composed detachment from the world is embodied no less by Shakespeare's Duke in *Measure for Measure* than by Marston's reconciled and restored Altofront in *The Malcontent* — while Altofront's other self, Malevole, gives voice to the stoic contempt for worldly ambition. Both are contrasted with Pietro, whose outlook combines the classical philosophy of sensuous discovery to which the stoical was opposed, the epicurean, with the pragmatism of Machiavelli (see p. xxvii, below) — although both schools of thought were misunderstood (or simply misrepresented) by their enemies. Not surprisingly, it is Pietro who makes a sneeringly explicit reference to Seneca, declaring that for all his stoic philosophy, he 'yet lived like a voluptuous epicure' (III, i, 27).

In the plays with which Marston followed *The Malcontent, The Dutch Courtesan* and *The Fawn*, his 'borrowings' included direct quotations from Montaigne, the French writer of the later sixteenth century who virtually invented the essay as a form of personal literary reflection. So John Florio's translation into English of Montaigne's collected *Essays,* published in 1603, presumably appeared just *after* Marston had completed *The Malcontent* — though some critics believe Shakespeare must have seen them in manuscript earlier, while he was writing *Hamlet*. Certainly, the spirit of tolerant scepticism and judicious enquiry which informs the *Essays* was sympathetic to Shakespeare, and the appearance of the work, whether recent or imminent, formed an important part of the intellectual ferment in which Marston was also working.

Plot and development

Virtually no act or scene divisions were marked in the separate, quarto editions of those of Shakespeare's plays published before the collected First Folio of 1623, and even in that edition the practice was inconsistent: thus, the divisions in modern editions of Shakespeare are not his own, but those imposed by later editors, and retained for convenience of reference. Whether or not Shakespeare thought or worked in terms of acts is a matter of critical debate. But in the private playhouses such as the Blackfriars, for which *The Malcontent* was originally written, the music played between the acts meant that the dramatist had to be more conscious of such breaks, and could use them as dramatic 'punctuation marks' if he so wished — whereas the 'not-received custom of music' (Ind., 84) at the open-air Globe (at least until *c.* 1607) caused Marston to flesh out his action with additional dialogue when the play was performed there (see further p. xxii, below).

The act divisions of our text thus follow those of the original quarto editions of 1604. So, too, do the scene divisions — but these fall in accordance with the neoclassical convention, also followed by Ben Jonson, of marking a new scene not after a clearance of the stage, or change of time or place (the practice generally followed by Shakespeare's editors), but with a change in the composition of the main characters. Thus, although the first act has no less than eight scenes, there are only two general clearances of the stage (after the soliloquies which close Scenes v and vii), and no apparent changes of location or other breaks in the flow of the action. The student should thus not allow the scene-divisions to disrupt his sense of the continuity of the action, but should consider how far they may represent structural 'units' (perhaps, as Marston's editor G.K. Hunter has suggested, as a new 'phrase' does in music) — and should sense also how the function and effect of the act-divisions would have changed when the play was expanded for its move from private to public theatre. There is no known source for the plot.

The Induction

A member of the audience gets into an argument with the property-man when he tries to sit on the stage, as was permitted at the private theatres but not here at the Globe. He is joined by his cousin, and the pair get into a discussion with three of the actors about the nature of the play they are about to see, and the changes that have been made for its production in the public playhouse. Although unfamiliar to modern audiences, an 'Induction' was not infrequently used as a sort of bridge between the everyday world and the play proper, for which it serves as a kind of picture-frame. (See further p. xxiv, below.)

Act One, Scenes One and Two
Discordant music is heard from the room of Malevole, a malcontent apparently living on the sufferance of Duke Pietro at the Genoese court, and two of the Duke's officers order the foul air to be perfumed before his arrival. Malevole, summoned following the Duke's appearance, roundly abuses the company, Pietro declaring that he tolerates his presence as a corrective to the flattery of others. As well as linking the noisy, smelly world of the playhouse with that of the play, these opening scenes quickly establish both the misanthropic temper of Malevole, and why his licensed railery has secured him a place in this otherwise sycophantic court.

Act One, Scene Three
Having sought a private word with the Duke, Malevole taunts Pietro with the claim that he is a cuckold. The Duke vows to have his revenge — and Malevole, in soliloquy, reveals that he, too, is seeking vengeance through the freedom his disguise has given him. The audience thus learns that Malevole has an ulterior motive for his behaviour (soon to be more fully revealed) through the first of the ironic parallels in which the action abounds.

Act One, Scenes Four and Five
From Malevole's encounter with his one faithful friend, Celso, we learn that he is truly the Duke Altofront — usurped when Pietro won the support of the Duke of Florence by marrying Florence's daughter, while Altofront's own wife was imprisoned in the citadel. He urges Celso that they should bide their time, and at once reverts to his Malevole-persona when the Duke's marshal, Bilioso, appears with a present from the grateful Pietro. He is followed by Mendoza, once the intermediary between Pietro and the Duke of Florence, but now cuckolding his own master: after some banter with Malevole, Mendoza reflects in soliloquy on the sweetness of being in favour with a prince — and with a prince's wife. As well as

establishing the intimate connection between political and sexual fidelity (and infidelity) these scenes further elaborate the intrigues in which the court is enmeshed, and clarify the motives of Altofront-Malevole and Celso as they await the opportunity for their own revenge.

Act One, Scenes Six and Seven

The old bawd Maquerelle tells the Duchess, Aurelia, that Mendoza now lusts after one of the Duchess's own ladies, Emilia. The enraged Aurelia instantly transfers her favours to another ardent admirer, Ferneze, and spurns the astonished Mendoza when he appears, leaving him to rail against the inconstancy of women. Challenged by the Duke, his sword drawn, Mendoza manages to divert suspicion from himself to Ferneze, promising to catch him that night in the very act of cuckoldry. Truth and falsehood now become ever more difficult to disentangle, though it is clear that Mendoza is skilled at turning the spiralling deceptions to his own advantage.

Act One, Scene Eight

Malevole encounters the Duke's fool, Passarello, a character who did not appear in the play as first performed (see page xxii, below). The ensuing repartee between the two 'professional' misanthropists serves not only as an interlude for wry reflection on the main action, but also to anticipate the enlarged role that Bilioso — once Passarello's master — is to play in the revised version.

Act Two, Scenes One, Two and Three

Mendoza gloats in soliloquy on the revenge he is taking against his rival and his former mistress. Malevole encounters Maquerelle walking with the Duchess's ladies — among them the beautiful young Bianca, whom he taunts for marrying the elderly and foolish Bilioso. When the women leave, Mendoza reappears in company with the Duke. Pietro receives the rough edge of the malcontent's tongue before turning him out, in order to complete his plans for the discovery of Ferneze. He swears his associates to secrecy — and names the 'deserving' Mendoza as his heir. In these short, contrasting scenes, the multiplicity of exits and entrances heightens the impression of a fast-unfolding plot in which all the events are apparently moving Mendoza's way.

Act Two, Scene Four

Maquerelle and her ladies discuss the best diet for sustaining beauty and wit — encouraging the bawd to inveigh against the good

fortune of men who grow wiser with the years while women lose
their beauty. The scene takes place in ironic counterpoint to the
love-making of Ferneze and Aurelia, from whose nearby room
come the strains of sweet music.

Act Two, Scene Five

Mendoza's scheme seems to be developing as planned: the surprised
Ferneze flees straight onto the point of his rapier, and the Duke,
declaring himself sated with revenge, departs. Mendoza is thus able
to make his peace with Aurelia, whom he persuades to conspire
with him against her husband's life, so that they may seize the
dukedom for themselves. When Aurelia leaves, Mendoza befriends
Malevole, now banished from court — but after Mendoza's
departure, Ferneze stirs into life, and is helped away by the
malcontent, who sees his own plot now beginning to work out.
Already, the seemingly tragic drift of the play is becoming
ambiguous, as the single character whom the audience believes
dead is brought quickly back to life — opportunely for Altofront-
Malevole, whose role now begins to appear omniscient rather than
merely manipulative.

Act Three, Scene One

Duke Pietro, melancholic after the discovery of his wife's infidelity,
gives Bilioso the task of informing the Duke of Florence of his
daughter's misconduct. Proud of the trust bestowed in him, Bilioso
boasts to his wife Bianca and the fool Passerello about the figure
he will cut in the Florentine court. This scene includes (lines
34-150) the longest of the interpolated episodes (see p. xxii, below),
in which Bilioso's transparent sense of self-importance forms an
apposite contrast to the no less fallible ambitions of the main
characters.

Act Three, Scene Two and Three

Malevole learns from Bilioso of his mission, and rails against all
courts and courtiers: but when he is alone with his confidant
Celso, the two agree that any intervention by Florence can only be
to their advantage, at a time when popular opinion is also beginning
to turn against Pietro. Mendoza appears, to conspire with the
supposedly disaffected Malevole against the Duke — whom
Malevole pretends to agree to murder. Mendoza declares that he
will then forsake Aurelia, and marry Altofront's imprisoned wife
Maria, in order to unite the opposing factions. With these scenes,
which interweave plot and counter-plot at an unrelenting pace, we

reach the mid-point of the play, and also, in the opinion of Altofront-Malevole and Celso, the turning-point in their own fortunes.

Act Three, Scenes Four and Five
After a brief interlude between Duke Pietro, out hunting, and his precocious page, Malevole appears, armed with Mendoza's own weapons, to alert Pietro to his danger — and to berate him for his folly in making his enemy his heir. He persuades the Duke to put on the disguise of a holy hermit, and to do as he is bid — heightening our sense that Altofront-Malevole has become not so much agent as 'presenter' of the unfolding action.

Act Four, Scenes One and Two
Maquerelle relates the events of the night to the Duchess's ladies, claiming that the lessons to be learned have to do not with fidelity but discretion. When the Duchess appears, she is intent only on dancing, and is displeased by the arrival of courtiers enquiring anxiously after the missing Duke. An air of heedless frivolity is now created, to contrast with the scene of the Duke's disabusing just past, and the further serious scene to follow.

Act Four, Scene Three
Malevole interrupts the dancing with news of the Duke's death — while the Duke himself, in his hermit's disguise, claims to have overheard his dying lament upon his dishonour, and to have seen him throw himself into the sea. Celso leads the court in proclaiming Mendoza as Duke, whereupon Mendoza condemns Aurelia to share the hermit's lot and, as soon as the others leave, dispatches Malevole to woo Altofront's 'grave duchess' Maria on his behalf. He then tempts the 'hermit' to poison Malevole, intending to lay the blame on Maria and so enforce her compliance. But when Malevole returns he is told to poison the hermit, for the same reason — Mendoza in soliloquy declaring that both must die, since he cannot afford to be beholden to such allies. Knowing, as we do, of the trust now existing between Malevole and Pietro, we realize that these criss-crossing threats carry little danger, but contribute rather to our sense of Mendoza's overweening evil, mounting now to a kind of self-nourishing absurdity.

Act Four, Scenes Four and Five
Having revealed Mendoza's orders to each other, Malevole and the disguised Pietro greet a distressed and penitent Aurelia. They then hear from the returned Bilioso that the Duke of Florence has

decreed that Aurelia should die — and that Pietro himself should be banished in favour of the Duke he usurped. On being told of Pietro's 'death', Bilioso determines to support whichever of Mendoza or Altofront shall prove the stronger. Alone again with Malevole, Pietro renounces his own claim, whereupon the malcontent reveals his identity. Not only events but the repentance of his former enemies continue to conspire in favour of Altofront, and to focus our attention upon Mendoza as the true villain of the piece.

Act Five, Scenes One and Two

Passarello engages Bilioso in clownly repartee, and then joins in more pointed banter with Malevole and Maquerelle — who, learning that the malcontent is to plead Mendoza's cause to the Duchess Maria, bemoans the mood of chastity which prevailed under her influence at court. The low verbal comedy in these scenes provides a necessary break after the gravity of the previous scene, and more importantly prepares us for the serious encounter with Maria which follows.

Act Five, Scene Three

Much to Maquerelle's disgust, Maria resolutely defends her honour against the blandishments and threats conveyed by Malevole, who, for the first time in our hearing, bemoans in an aside the necessity of continuing to play his role as malcontent. There is a harsh edge, too, to his treatment of Bilioso, who seeks the favours of this supposed new favourite in vain — his unabashed time-serving juxtaposed with the Duchess's incorruptible constancy.

Act Five, Scene Four

Malevole pretends to Mendoza that the 'hermit' is safely poisoned — whereupon Mendoza, using the box of poisons shown to him by the malcontent, proceeds to dispose (as he thinks) of this other too-knowing servant. He instructs Celso to see Malevole buried, then to prepare a masque in celebration of his instalment — which Malevole determines to join. Although the idea of such a celebration apparently occurs to Mendoza on the spur of the moment, it is at once incorporated into the plans which (as Altofront now tells Celso) are about to reach their culmination.

Act Five, Scenes Five and Six

Maquerelle and the ladies comment on the qualities of the courtiers as they assemble for the masque under Bilioso's bustling direction. Upon Mendoza's entrance, he confronts Maria and, failing to move her, accuses her of responsibility for the death of the hermit. The distraught Aurelia enters, and is silenced as the masque begins. Among the masquers, Malevole and the 'hermit' dance with their own wives, revealing their true identities first to the ladies — and then to Mendoza, as they unmask before him. The whole company acclaims Altofront as Duke, Mendoza receives the mercy he pleads for, and the restored Duke deals summarily but not harshly with all his former enemies — a climax which stresses both the comic, reconciliatory nature of the play, and also, in its rather perfunctory quality, the fact that our pleasure depends on seeing a pattern completed rather than on a sense of justice triumphant.

Commentary

The structure of the play

There is more to the 'structure' of a play than is imposed by its
division into acts and scenes — more relevant though act-divisions
are to *The Malcontent* than to contemporary plays conceived for
the public theatres. Still less is structure simply to do with putting-
together a coherent plot. Indeed, the 'plot' of *The Malcontent* is
relatively straightforward compared with the private-theatre plays
Jonson was writing for the boy players around this time, and there
is no sub-plot as such, though the Bilioso-Passarello-Maquerelle
level of behaviour at court is in some ways subordinate to the
Pietro-Mendoza level of action. But Malevole is usually present as
participant in and commentator upon the scenes involving both
sets of characters — who, when they overlap, as in the Ferneze-
Aurelia incident, can scarcely be sorted into 'main' and 'subsidiary'
participants. And the very isolation of the Ferneze-Aurelia affair
also suggests that its purpose is not to *forward* the plot, but rather
to illustrate a particular *kind* of behaviour.

Even Malevole is less instrumental than he at first proclaims
himself in forwarding his own ends: rather, events conspire to assist
him, adept though he is at turning them to advantage — whether in
the discovery that Ferneze is alive, the intervention of the Duke of
Florence, or the almost incidental revelation that public opinion
and the military are both finally declaring in his favour (V, iv,
90-2). Neither Duke nor populace make personal appearances in
the action, and Malevole himself describes such turns of events as
'a whirl of fate . . . tumbling on'. The stress in the play thus falls
less on his own machinations than on the patterns of human
behaviour in the corrupt court and the changes effected by a tragi-
comic resolution which is *itself* effected by the 'tumbling' of fate.

It is probably significant in this respect that Malevole (by
contrast with his better-known fellow malcontent, Hamlet)
seldom confides his own thoughts to the audience. He is allowed
only one soliloquy — the addition in Act I, Scene iii, which serves
a largely expository purpose — and apart from occasional 'asides'
he speaks before the climactic scenes largely under his assumed

identity (except, of course, to his confidant Celso, where disclosure is again functional to the plot rather than self-revelatory). How this 'privacy' affects our feelings about Malevole-Altofront is discussed elsewhere (see p. xxxii): here we need only note how it enhances his importance as 'presenter' of the action rather than participant.

The action itself thus tends to be broken into a sequence of *exempla* — more or less self-contained episodes illuminating satirical or moral points — with Malevole acting as a connecting-link between them. If, then, we think of his single soliloquy as ending the expository 'movement' of the play, the encounter with Bilioso which follows in Act I, Scene iv, may be seen as an *exemplum* in which the previously contemptuous old courtier tests out whether (and how far) Malevole's new-found favour with Pietro requires him to turn obsequious — while Malevole's 'aside' to Celso and the italicized *sententiae* (74-80) provide apt moral comments upon the incident. To view the structure of the play in this way, as purposefully episodic, also makes it easier to accept that the 'augmentations' which Marston provided for the Globe production, and which we shall now discuss, were not a sort of padding to the plot, but an enrichment of an existing formal pattern.

The effect of the 'augmentations'

There is no space here in which to sift all the evidence, circumstantial and stylistic, over the authorship of the additional dialogue written for the Globe production of *The Malcontent*. I am assuming that John Webster wrote the Induction (see p. xxiv, below); that Marston was himself responsible for all the 'augmentations' to the play proper; and that their purpose was largely to compensate for the hour or so of music which normally preceded plays at the private theatres, and for the musical interludes between the acts.

The Induction and augmentations together increased the length of the play by almost 600 lines to a total of just under 2,500 — which has been calculated as almost exactly the average length for a Globe play of the period. For that information I am indebted to G.K. Hunter's valuable introduction to his edition of the play, which also helpfully lists all the scenes and characters involved:

I, iii, 108-49	Malevole, Pietro
I, iii, 155-72	Malevole
I, iv, 43-89	Malevole, Bilioso

We note at once the absence of additions between Act III, Scene i, and Act V, Scene i, already the busiest and most densely-plotted section of the play. We notice, too, the prominence in these 'augmentations' of Bilioso and the fool Passarello — the latter a new character altogether, who serves, of course, as a further commentator upon the action, unequivocally comic where Malevole is ambiguously so. The additions in which they appear largely illustrate or castigate the extravagances of courtly behaviour, and, in serving as further *exempla* to Marston's satiric ends, so far from 'padding out' the action serve it more aptly than the musical entertainment they replaced. Of the few additions that are more serious in tone, the first, in which Malevole elaborates his views on adultery for Pietro's benefit, stresses the parallel between sexual and political aggrandisement which is elsewhere treated in a more comic light, and the second is the soliloquy discussed in the previous section. But to make such distinctions between the 'serious' and the 'comic' is to beg questions concerning the play's form, discussed more fully below (p. xxxi).

It is probably all the more helpful to look separately at the 'augmentations' if the reader has *not* found them disruptive to his sense of the structure of the play; but this, of course, may have been because a sense of *continuous* disruption is integral to Marston's intentions. Any such discussion of 'intentions' must remain conjectural, but it is surely more reasonable to assume that Marston was *aiming* for the effects he achieves (if we perceive them as having a coherent dramatic purpose) than to object, as does the critic L.G. Salingar, that 'Marston cannot submerge himself consistently in his play', and that 'the dramatist's pretence to objectivity' consequently 'breaks down'. Why *should* Marston submerge himself in his play? *Does* he pretend objectivity? But in these questions the play's structural qualities are again beginning to touch upon its form, to which we shall return in a later section (see p. xxxi, below).

The use of music
According to the historian of renaissance theatre music,
J.S. Manifold, Marston, 'more than any other dramatist, sets out to
link the act music with the play'. Since our text is intended for the
public theatre, where act music was not the custom, we have only
the stage direction which remains at the beginning of Act II to give
us an example of Marston integrating music and action; but we can
also see that, since the Induction would not have been played
in the original Blackfriars production, the hour or so's opening
music at that theatre would have been followed directly by the
'vilest out-of-tune music' which begins the play proper — and
which would have sounded all the more vile for the contrast!   The
public theatres were, however, by no means lacking in musical
resources, and many elements remain — of songs, at the opening of
Act I, Scene iii, of Act II, Scene iv, and in the interlude with the
First Page, a role presumably taken by one of the child apprentices
at the Globe (III, iv, 42); in the social dancing of Act IV; the
'music within' at II, iv, 53; and, of course, in the full-dress masque
which is integral to the climactic revelations. In reading the play it
is important to give some imaginative thought to reconstructing at
least the spirit of such musical ingredients, often indicated only by
a curt stage direction in the text, but in performance occupying
significant stage time, and contributing, emotionally rather than
intellectually, to the atmosphere of the scene.

Levels of theatricality
John Webster's Induction to *The Malcontent* is well worth the
effort of understanding — not as an irrelevant appendage made all
the more difficult (and all the more tempting to skip) by its
contemporary theatrical references, but as a 'way into' both the
theatre whose conditions it recreates and the world of the play
itself. Like the 'augmentations' just discussed, its addition to the
original text was intended to ease the move from a private to a
public playhouse. It did this not merely by further extending the
play's length to compensate for the 'not-received custom of music',
but also by substituting for the 'distancing effect' of boy players
simulating adult behaviour that of adult actors presenting
themselves in their own persons — one of their number, Will Sly,
even playing an audience member who proceeds to call for Harry
Condell, Dick Burbage . . . and also for Will Sly, who, as
everybody knew, was already there (11-13).
     Sly is playing a frequenter of the private theatres (where he is

permitted to sit on the stage) and clearly regards any playhouse more as a place of fashion than of entertainment. He has 'seen this play often', presumably in its earlier version, and has written down favourite quotations from it in his 'table-book', or commonplace book (see further p. xi, above). After exchanging a few bawdy remarks with his 'cousin' — another actor, John Sinklo — he asks how the company came by this play, and is told that it is now being performed by the adults in retaliation for the children having stolen one of the adult company's works — probably Kyd's still popular *Spanish Tragedy* (72-80). Sly boasts of his excellent memory for signs (see further p. xxix, below), and is finally persuaded to take one of the private boxes in the galleries, improvising a prologue for the play as he leaves.

Apart from the glimpses of the manners and customs of the playhouse that it gives us, the Induction establishes the world of the play as no less deliberately artificial than it was in the hands of the boys. Then, in the very first scene, the courtiers compare the noise and smells to those of a brothel-house — which in Elizabethan minds would not have been far from the playhouse. Burbage soon re-enters in his character of Malevole — itself, of course, an *assumed* character — with his recent appearance under his own name only a little fresher in the audience's minds than his last 'malcontent' role, that of Hamlet. Even at the end of the play, a masque serves (as in *The Spanish Tragedy*) to redouble disguises before it reveals them — and once Malevole has finally 'become' Duke Altofront, and disposed in summary fashion of friends and enemies alike, he makes a final transition to his 'real' identity as an actor in a none-too-subtle appeal for applause (V, vi, 165-7).

In between, most of the characters in the play are occupied with playing roles — Pietro not simply when he assumes the overt role of a hermit, but in his very usurpation of the dukedom; Bilioso in his constant adjustments of his behaviour to the shifting scale of royal favour; Maquerelle as supplier of sexual fantasies (compared by some critics to Genet's madam, Irma, in *The Balcony*); Mendoza, whether playacting in his manipulation of the Ferneze-Aurelia affair or in the sequence of deceptions which leads to his little brief authority; and, of course, the fool Passarello, whose very function is in part to serve as bridge between the world of the play and the world of the audience beyond.

One comparison which might be considered is between the parallel 'actual' and 'artificial' worlds of *The Malcontent* and the similarly parallel worlds of children's games — which are marked by the unselfconscious ease with which the participants step from pretence to reality and back again: an epic sea-voyage is interrupted by supper, a battle held up for an out-of-role debate on whose turn it is to be killed. To that extent, the original child actors in *The Malcontent* would readily enough have created the constantly ambiguous 'reality' of the play. The adult players of the Globe had to find their own ways of 'seeing' the play within the quotation-marks of 'let's pretend'. And for modern actors and audiences, distance in time adds further complexity to our response — in deciding, for example, when a convention is obtrusive simply because of its unfamiliarity, and when because Marston intended to stress the artificiality of the play as a play. As the modern German dramatist Brecht would have wished, such an emphasis can help to keep our critical senses alert: it can also, as Brecht's near-contemporary, the Italian writer Pirandello, believed, create a new sense of the ambiguity of 'reality', in which actors, characters, and audience conspire to transcend the sharp-edged logic of the everyday.

At the Globe, Burbage, who had played Hamlet wearing *his* mask or face of malcontent, began the play of that name by playing an actor of his own name who was about to play a deposed duke who was himself playing at being a malcontent — while the character whose speech ends the play is a duke who has just been playing another character being played by Malevole in a masque and who is now himself putting on the mask of benevolent ruler, but who turns out to be an actor named Burbage asking politely for an audience's applause. Such an awareness of the many levels of the action at least serves to 'distance' the play from any expectation that Malevole's feelings should be psychologically 'real', or Altofront's necessarily consistent with them.

The Italianate setting

In his introductory note 'To the Reader', Marston apologises for inventing a Dukedom of Genoa and makes clear that his characters are not based on the noble families of that Italian city. But his disavowals seem intended to deflect suspicions that the targets of his satire were altogether nearer home, and the defensive tone of the whole introduction suggests that parallels were indeed being drawn (and, despite Marston's protestations, probably intended) between the corrupt court of his play and the new King James's tendency to surround himself with favourites and to dispense places and honours in return for cash.

Marston's own half-Italian descent should, perhaps, have given him a more intimate knowledge than most of his contemporaries could claim of the country in which he set several other of his plays besides *The Malcontent:* in practice, his portrayal of it is no less impressionistic. But there were good practical and artistic reasons why Italy nonetheless provided a setting for so much Jacobean tragedy. From there in 1520 had come what was still regarded as virtually a handbook of political intrigue — *The Prince,* by the statesman and philosopher Machiavelli, whose very name had become, somewhat unjustly, synonymous with devious (and probably devilish) conspiracy. Italy itself was still divided into self-governing city states — most importantly, Milan, Venice, and Florence, in whose sphere of influence Marston incorrectly situates his Genoa — and into the kingdoms of Naples, Sicily, and Sardinia. And the constant rivalries and disputes caused by this fragmentation, often involving alliances with stronger foreign powers such as France and Spain, were heightened by the presence of the papacy, not only as a contentious spiritual authority but as a temporal force governing a large area around Rome. The most accessible source for English knowledge of recent Italian affairs was a *History of Italy* by the early sixteenth century statesman Guicciardini, some of which had appeared in translation in the *Chronicles* of Holinshed. In English eyes, Guicciardini's 'realistic' approach to the intrigues of the Medicis only served to confirm the alignment they already suspected between Italian politics and the tenets of Machiavelli.

But Italy had also, of course, been the birthplace of the Renaissance, the 'rebirth' of the classical art and learning of Ancient Greece and Rome, whose influence spread throughout western Europe between the fourteenth and the sixteenth century — incidentally contributing, in the short prose narrative form of the *novella,* source material for many Elizabethan and Jacobean plays. Although there is no such known source, literary or historical, for *The Malcontent,* the play is saturated with that sense of a 'mythical' Italy to which all the above influences and perceptions contributed — a nation whose classical heritage lent it immense cultural authority and contributed to the continuing flowering of its art, yet whose political intrigues were, whether through the officially detested power of the Catholic religion or the supposedly quite irreligious influence of Machiavelli, at once alien and compulsively fascinating to English writers and audiences alike.

The language of the play

In the late fifteen-eighties the dramatist Christopher Marlowe had made 'blank verse' the distinctive vehicle for Elizabethan tragedy — unrhymed lines of ten syllables, divided into five feet with the stress generally falling on the second syllable of each. By the turn of the new century, Shakespeare and his contemporaries were beginning to explore more flexible uses of blank verse — by means of lines which were not 'end-stopped', by changes in the expected emphasis, by subtle manipulation of the 'caesura' (a sort of 'felt pause' in each line), by deliberate irregularities or metre, and a variety of other devices intended to keep the verse in tune with the constantly changing dramatic needs of a play.

Marston, though much criticized and satirized for his alleged clumsiness of style, was also helping to expand the boundaries of what blank verse as a medium could encompass. We need not disagree with the critic Theodore Spencer that his style represented 'a kind of growing pain which language was bound to suffer as it passed from the manner of Spenser to the manner of Donne', but we should question the implication that Marston's experimental approach amounted to a sort of linguistic adolescence.

Of course, much of *The Malcontent* is in prose, not verse, but this is not for the usual purpose of distinguishing between 'high' and 'low' scenes, since shifts backwards and forwards occur not only *within* scenes of both kinds, but within the speeches of individual characters. Indeed, Marston's style has such a jagged fluidity (to employ a Marstonian sort of phrase, strained but provocative) that editors sometimes have difficulty in deciding the form in which to print it. Marston's introductory message 'To the Reader' even apologises for his play's 'ungainly shape' on the page, but reminds us that it was intended to be 'presented with the soul of lively action' — or, as he put it in a similar note to *The Fawn*, 'Comedies are writ to be spoken, not read: remember the life of these things consists in action'. Considered as an acting medium, as Marston here advises, the language of the play reflects with its own perverse decorum the shifts of mood which the players are required to express. Thus, Marston's editor G.K. Hunter has persuasively suggested that 'Verse often grows out of prose as a point of view crystallizes out of disordered facts and then breaks down into prose again when passion overcomes the ordered vision of verse.' This is probably as good a general guideline as any: but the actor who works *with* the language may find that no guideline is required once the words are spoken rather than read.

We tend today to put less emphasis than was once fashionable on strains of imagery in a play, once believed to provide, as Una Ellis-Fermor expressed it, 'the essential indications of mood and underlying thought' — a main vehicle of 'psychological analysis, particularly self-analysis', which she believed Marston to have achieved in the character of Malevole after his earlier 'derivative' work. Certainly the student may trace for himself in *The Malcontent* a pervasive imagery of *hunting,* or 'the chase', which contributes, at an almost subliminal level (until we ourselves go 'hunting' for it) to our sense of the 'tone of voice' in which a character speaks. And this is one of several ways in which Marston *controls* language, even when his characters appear most *out* of control.

As the frequency with which he coined words and phrases new to the language (neologisms) also suggests, Marston was profoundly conscious of language and its effects — as were most of his contemporaries, for whom the sermon and the well-turned legal plea often had no less attraction than the play, and were to be no less admired for their rhetorical skill. But Marston is less typical in that his characters often seem to *share* his fascination, indulging (if I may employ a coinage of my own) in a sort of 'meta-rhetoric', or language which comments on its own use. Thus, a fine speech will be given a 'throwaway' tag which undercuts its carefully developed effect, or a character will deflate a preceding speech with a sharp point of linguistic criticism. Combined with his frequent employment of *sententiae* (see p. xi, above) — which would have demanded a kind of spoken emphasis equivalent to the italics which distinguish them in our text — such self-referential language must have required an acting approach in which verbal and gestic components inextricably blended to produce a play 'writ to be spoken not read'.

The visual dimension
In Webster's Induction to *The Malcontent,* the self-important spectator played by Will Sly boasts that he can 'walk but once down by the Goldsmiths' Row in Cheap, take notice of the signs, and tell you them with a breath instantly' (Ind, 105-7). The signs 'begin as the world did, with Adam and Eve', and would all, of course, have been pictorial — like the British inn-signs which are the last, pleasantly archaic remnant of a tradition which derived from the need to locate addresses in a recognizable way for a largely illiterate population. Thus, although most members of

Marston's audience would not have been able to read, they would
have shared, if not quite to the same degree, Will Sly's gift of
visual 'literacy' — an alertness to even the most meagre visual data,
in the same way that we might almost instinctively take note today
of the slogan flashed by a passing poster, or the destination board
of a bus.

The Elizabethan and Jacobean theatre attached little importance
to scenic embellishments beyond one or two basic properties —
such as the throne of state with its raised dais, which the stage
directions interestingly do *not* stipulate for the final act, or a grand
four-poster bed (again, *not* required in the second act, since
Marston tactfully takes us only as far as the ante-chamber to
Aurelia's bedroom). And while masques at court were given lavish
scenic trappings, none are indicated for the last-act masque in *The
Malcontent*. In short, Marston was happy for his audience largely
to depend on his own words and the capabilities of the players to
'locate' his action — a reminder, perhaps, that a paradoxical virtue
of illiteracy may be the ability to 'translate' the contents of spoken
words and images directly into the pictures they conjure up,
instead of 'seeing' them first through a haze of 'mental print'.

My use of quotation marks when using familiar words in
unfamiliar ways for the processes I am describing suggests how
tentative our terminology must be in this area, if we are to avoid
the too-often-mystifying jargon of semiotic analysis — which has,
however, been helpful in stressing how many aspects of a play in
performance *signify meaning* in addition to the words uttered by
the actors. Dress is perhaps the most obvious example — and we
know from such evidence as inventories and account books of the
period that considerable expenditure was lavished on costuming
the actors. We are given some hints of Marston's own requirements
in the stage directions to *The Malcontent* in which clothes often
'make the man' indeed (even hats enjoying a social significance,
as the discussion in the Induction on the etiquette of their removal
and on the functions of feathered plumage ironically reminds us)

Dumb-shows also played their part in conveying non-verbal
meaning — and the stage direction which opens Act II (presumably
a relic of the Blackfriars performance in its instruction for actors
to enter 'whilst the act is playing') gives brief instructions for one
such. Marston's editor Bernard Harris comments on the use of
'attendants, pages, lights, ladies, processions, music, dancing, . . .
masque . . . costume and jewellery, the preparation of food and the
customs of the chase', in a convenient inventory of the range of

If so, the audience will, surely, *share the joke* with Malevole. And supposedly 'difficult' moments, such as Ferneze's return from the dead (II, v, 136-61), as also the recurrent occasions when 'high' and 'low' characters converge in Malevole's presence, lose much of their problematic quality if we, as audience, recognize with Malevole that absurd events and contingencies *are* absurd — both in the comic *and* the existential meanings of the term.

Such an approach does not require us to invent some such latter-day label as 'tragi-comedy of the absurd', but simply to keep Marston's own comic distance from his subject and his central character. The original Blackfriars audience was already 'distanced' by the staging conditions discussed earlier: and so it is surely significant, from the generic as well as the structural viewpoint, that, for the less sophisticated audiences of the Globe, Marston chose to nudge the play further towards the *comic* end of the formal spectrum. In my view, Malevole is no more Marston than Hamlet was Shakespeare. But Malevole *is* in part Hamlet — or rather, is Hamlet wearing his own mask of the malcontent, and like Hamlet (and probably like Burbage, playing them both) at times identifying with his role, at times intellectualizing it, but always the professional performer, manipulating fellow-characters and audience alike.

The characters: 'acting' and 'personation'
The belief that the portrayal of 'individuality' is of overriding artistic interest dates only from the romantic revival of the later eighteenth century, before which it was a more usual aim for art to represent what was *typical* in human behaviour — including, of course, what was 'typically' eccentric. Such 'truth to type' was the essence of the neoclassical concept of 'decorum' in comic drama, and was also expressed through the popular Jacobean prose form of 'character writing' — collections of brief sketches which represented their subjects either as the personification of universal vices and virtues, or as exemplifying a particular social or political affectation of the day. Ben Jonson's early 'humours' technique was essentially a comic variation on this approach: based on the old medical belief that the human temperament was subject to the balance of the four 'humours', or bodily fluids, it drew its characters as governed by a 'predominant passion' such as lust, greed, or ambition.

The word 'acting' was first used to describe the *gestic* component among the *orator's* skills, and it was possibly Marston himself who

coined the term 'personation' (in the Induction to his earlier
Antonio and Mellida) to suggest that the actor's art should include
character-drawing as well as the simple declamation of a role. But
the sheer size and quick turnover of the repertoire of plays
performed by any acting company required players to develop
'lines' of roles in which they could specialize: and even the use of
the definite article in the title of *The Malcontent* suggests the
extent to which the play was dealing in such *theatrical* 'types', as
well as in 'characters' in the specific Jacobean sense. The roles in
the play thus make up in artistic complexity whatever they lack in
psychological. (At the same time, many modern actors will
approach their roles according to the techniques of a Stanislavski-
based training, and so will try to 'discover' a biographical
background and a psychological make-up which the historical
critic refuses to admit.)

So central is the nature of 'the malcontent' himself to the way
we perceive this play, that almost no section of this commentary
fails to touch upon some aspect of the 'character'. The other most
recognizable 'type' is, of course, the fool Passarello — the single
role added in the 'augmentations', and one which presumably
utilized the services of the clown then playing with the King's Men,
Robert Armin, whose other recent parts would have included
Touchstone in *As You Like It* and Feste in *Twelfth Night*. The
fawning old courtier Bilioso would also have been recognized as of
the same type as Polonius in *Hamlet* — at once a caricature of
the 'true Castilio' he would wish himself (after Castiglione, author
of *The Courtier*), and in that long line of foolish old gentlemen
which stretches back to the plays of Plautus and beyond. Marston's
editor Bernard Harris, pointing out that other characters in *The
Malcontent* are named from Florio's *A World of Words* (1598),
raises 'the possibility that this paraded life might be typified in the
fashion of the morality tradition' — and suggests, for example, that
Maquerelle 'offers "a bawd or a pander", as well as "mackrel" and
"a ravenous fowl".' However, as he concedes, there is little
consistency in the approach to nomenclature, and Marston's use of
it 'is perhaps only part of a larger activity involving the creation of
further inhabited worlds seen as extensions of the play-world'.
Thus, he instances 'the names which spring readily to Malevole's
lips throughout the play' as being 'associated with notions of
sexual appetite'.

Marston breaks rules as readily as observing them. There is no
true 'consistency' in the characterization of his leading villains, of

whom Pietro becomes a penitent while Mendoza is transformed from a sensual opportunist into a cold Machiavellian intriguer. It would be difficult indeed to find adequate 'psychological' explanations for their behaviour, but it 'works' dramatically within the exemplary world of the play. I am not therefore attempting here the brief 'character sketches' offered in other volumes in this series. In the last analysis, character operates in this play as a function of plot, and within the web of conventions and expectations of the age — both about human behaviour as such, and how it might be reflected in a play.

Themes and conventions

The revenge tradition

Although *The Malcontent* is not strictly a play about revenge, it does owe something to that recurrent theme of Elizabethan and Jacobean drama. Derived from the Senecan influence already discussed, its use can be traced from one of the period's very earliest successes, Kyd's *The Spanish Tragedy* (*c.* 1589), through *Hamlet* (*c.* 1601), to Tourneur's *The Revenger's Tragedy* (1607), Chapman's *The Revenge of Bussy D'Ambois* (1610), and beyond. Marston himself had tried his hand at revenge tragedy in *Antonio's Revenge* (1600), in which he included one familiar feature of the type — the ghost calling for his wrongs to be avenged, who is conspicuously absent from *The Malcontent* since Altofront, unlike most avengers, is seeking to set right an injustice done to himself. But it is relevant to note, as did the critic Helen Gardner regarding *Hamlet,* that most avengers are *not* directly successful in their plans: rather, as she points out, 'The revenger takes an opportunity unconsciously provided for him by the villain. Given the opportunity, which he seems unable to create for himself, he forms his scheme on the spur of the moment.' This certainly reminds us how Malevole's initial plan to avenge his political usurpation by revealing the sexual usurpation of Aurelia is so effortlessly thwarted by Mendoza — whose *own* scheme for Ferneze's death, however, provides Malevole with one of his several 'spur-of-the-moment' opportunities.

Just as Hamlet fails to kill Claudius when presented with an ideal occasion, so too — and at exactly the same stage of the play — Malevole fails to kill Pietro when, fully armed, he finds him sleeping (III, iv-v). And arguably it is only Mendoza's compulsive need to compound his initial crimes — by conspiring with his supposed accomplices to kill each other, and by forsaking Aurelia for the expedient of marriage with Maria — that is his undoing. Thus, Mendoza (like Claudius in *Hamlet,* conspiring against his nephew) is ultimately destroyed by himself — except, of course, that in this case it is only his ambitions which are destroyed, while he himself is forgiven. Malevole, like Hamlet, has seized rather than created his opportunities for revenge — though unlike Hamlet he does not die in the moment of his success, but lives to enjoy it (even if the nature of that 'enjoyment', as often in tragi-comedy, is not easy to envisage).

Helen Gardner further pointed out that whereas in *The Spanish Tragedy* Kyd's Hieronimo is transformed by his vengeful intentions from a just and honest man into a man of blood who 'becomes as crafty as his enemy', Hamlet is able to preserve his moral integrity. Interestingly, through the device of the dual-personality, Marston presents us with *both* the crafty conspirator that Malevole (not altogether successfully) has become, *and* the guiltless 'instrument' that is the restored Altofront. The role of villain, too, is split — between the original usurper Pietro, and the newly-conspiring Mendoza. And so, while Hamlet fails to kill Claudius because, since he is at his prayers, he may save his soul, Malevole fails to kill Pietro because he *wants* to save his soul — thus, arguably, turning revenge tragedy into revenge comedy. Theatrically, of course, the reasons are identical in both cases: there are still two full acts of the play to run! As in most matters of theatrical convention, dramatic and structural necessity are inseparable.

Anatomy of the 'malcontent'

As Marston's choice of title confirms, the condition of being 'malcontented' is of more crucial concern to his play than the theme of revenge — and is also closer to everyday Jacobean life, in which 'revenge' was, confessedly, a rather exceptional pursuit outside the theatre. But the state of being a 'malcontent' was quite a fashionable one — an expression of the supposed predominance of the 'humour' of black bile in the system, whose effects Robert Burton was to celebrate in *The Anatomy of Melancholy* in 1621.

In terms of the sense of malaise specific to our period (see p. ix, above), Marston's biographer Philip J. Finkelpearl has described *The Malcontent* as the dramatist's 'most successful representation of a morally debilitated world'. Finkelpearl also believed that in Marston's time 'the title would have had political connotations', and certainly 'malcontent' was one of the terms applied to the recently disaffected (and beheaded) Earl of Essex. But D.J. Palmer sees the type as the embodiment of 'the new tragic hero' — a description which fits Hamlet well enough, as, more arguably, it does Malevole himself and such a figure as Flamineo in Webster's *The White Devil* (1612), but is scarcely appropriate to such non-tragic 'malcontents' as Thersites in *Troilus and Cressida*, Jaques in *As You Like It*, Macilente in Jonson's *Every Man out of His Humour*, or Malheureux in Marston's own *The Dutch Courtesan*. And the issue is further complicated by the suggestion that Marston may himself have been the real-life prototype for Jaques and Thersites — a piece of hearsay which, whether or not it happens to be true, at least reminds us that this is a type drawn as much from life as art.

Theodore Spencer makes a distinction between malcontents like Hamlet and Marston's own Antonio, whose melancholy is turned inward by a grief that has soured their faith in human nature, and those, like Malevole or Flamineo, who feel themselves 'displaced persons' in the social order, satirically lashing but also perversely revelling in the corruption they see around them. One might add that some of the comic malcontents, and perhaps Malevole too, fulfil something of the role more traditionally taken by fools of the wittier kind: it is, at least, rather in these terms that Malevole is introduced into the play by Pietro — as one who is 'as free as air; he blows over every man', and who 'gives good intelligence to my spirit, makes me understand those weaknesses which others' flattery palliates' (I, ii, 28-iii, 3). Earlier in the same passage, Malevole has also been said to 'afflict all in that to which they are most affected' — a technique which, functionally, serves to initiate the series of *exempla* in which Malevole is as much *provocateur* as participant. It also aligns not only the malcontent's own character but those he 'afflicts' within the 'humours' tradition of the early Ben Jonson, which delineated characters by their predominant passions.

In so self-aware a play, it would be surprising if a malcontent elevated to the ironic dignity of title character (ironic, since that 'character' is ostensibly a mask for Altofront) was not at some level commenting upon the theatrical type itself, as well as reflecting a persona fashionable in life. It is in this light, I think, that we should read the oft-quoted passage at Act III, Scene ii, 1-14 — which is not so much an attempt by Malevole at self-definition as a *performance,* for the benefit of Bilioso. Malevole, of course, is not alone among malcontents in regarding the world as a stage on which to perform for others: when Jaques in *As You Like It* delivers his set speech, 'All's the world a stage' (II, vii, 139-66), he, too, is putting on an act — and delivering not a string of Shakespearian pearls of wisdom, but of well-worn clichés through which Shakespeare reveals the character's self-indulgent conventionality. That he does so within the familiar metaphor of the world as a stage is very much to Shakespeare's point about the self-dramatizing quality of the malcontent.

The politics of sexuality

As we have already noted, the first step in Malevole's plan to reclaim his dukedom is to reveal to the usurper Pietro that *he* has been usurped in his role as a husband. The play ends with the usurped duke forgiving the usurper, and the wronged husband forgiving the unfaithful wife. And throughout the action Marston illustrates the close parallels between sexual and political ambition — contrasting it (perhaps none too forcefully in terms of dramatic emphasis) with the faith kept between Maria and Altofront. Similarly, in the 'argument' to his later comedy, *The Dutch Courtesan,* Marston claims that 'the full scope of the play' consists in 'the difference between the love of a courtesan and a wife' — but allows all the theatrical, if not all the moral stress to fall on the courtesan. (Although prostitution had ostensibly been put down in London, as Malevole remarks (V, iv, 30-4), the whores remained near neighbours to the players in the Bankside 'entertainment district' — ironically, often as tenants of property owned by the Church.)

In *The Dutch Courtesan* Marston explored his sexual theme with a thematic and linguistic directness unusual even in those sexually explicit times — to the extent that some critics have suspected in him a fascinated repulsion, akin to Swift's, for the closeness not only of lust and love, but of the excretory and sexual functions. In *The Malcontent,* certainly, we are never far from the brothel, since the court itself appears to keep a resident bawd, in the person of the 'old panderess' Maquerelle — who is finally sent back to 'the suburbs' where the 'stews' of the time flourished (V, vi, 162). But so far from merely providing bawdy 'light relief', her role is often central to the main action. In Act I, Scene vi, for example, her intervention on Ferneze's behalf is placed carefully between Mendoza's long soliloquy in the previous scene — in which his luxuriant delight at being a political favourite turns with sensuous fluency to his pleasure in the enjoyment of women —

and his contrasting expression of disillusioned disgust after being displaced in Aurelia's affections (I, vi, 80-97). Maquerelle acts again as a 'go-between' in a structural as well as a sexual sense in Act II, Scene iv, where her meeting with Bianca and Emila separates the scene in which Pietro and Mendoza plot to kill Ferneze from the implementation of that plan: meanwhile Aurelia and Ferneze are in the throes of their illicit passion.

Contemporary feminist criticism alerts us to the dangers of a typology which separates sexually-desirable women into immaculate madonnas (such as Maria) and whores (such as Aurelia) — judging them, in short, purely in terms of their 'value' as intact or 'soiled' sexual commodities. However, it would be unhistorical not to acknowledge also the economic basis of the male fear of cuckoldry (so expertly played on by Malevole in Act I, Scene iii, 77-151), at a time when inheritance (and its legitimacy) was of almost mystical importance. And, of course, it is precisely the 'legitimacy' of the dukedom which Pietro has usurped — and which, in turn, Mendoza hopes to restore by marrying the 'true' duchess and casting off his 'illicit' mistress. He 'loves' Maria, he says, 'as wise men do love great women, to ennoble their blood and augment their revenue' (III, iii, 102-4). There is, perhaps, nothing very unusual in this frank expression of the politics of Jacobean sexuality — until one contrasts Marston's plays with Shakespeare's, in which the sense of a strong link between the lust for sex and power is so exceptional as to be one reason why the 'problem plays' (which *do* express it) are thought problematic.

The wheel of fortune

A medieval concept, the 'wheel of fortune' was still regarded in the Tudor period as emblematic of the way in which the goddess Fortune restored her whimsical version of balance — or, simply, demonstrated her inconstancy. The wheel bore up the aspirant to a peak from which, inevitably, he began to fall — while another behind was rising in his place. The modern critic George L. Geckle saw the wheel of fortune as a 'symbol around which both the structure of the play and its most serious themes literally revolve'; but (quite apart from the question of how a structure can 'literally' revolve around a symbol) this seems to me to overstate the significance of the concept for Marston — at least to judge from the references to it in his text. As ever with *The Malcontent,* one also has to consider how far such references *reflect upon* the idea, rather than simply reflecting it.

Thus, when Malevole asks Maquerelle how she regards the 'transformation of state' that has replaced Pietro with Mendoza, she replies that 'we women always note the falling of the one is the rising of the other' — the proverbial phrase in the old bawd's mouth carrying clear sexual rather than cyclical connotations. Maquerelle goes on to liken the behaviour of Lady Fortune to her own inconstancy towards two pet lapdogs (V, ii, 40-55). And when Malevole himself refers to the ways of the goddess, he compares them to two buckets in a well: 'whilst one comes up full to be emptied, another goes down empty to be filled' (III, iii, 63-6).

Certainly, as we've already noted, Malevole attributes his own ascendant fortunes to the 'tumbling' of fate (V, iv, 90-2), and the play's climax is presented as dependent more upon the whims of popular and military opinion — not to mention the support of that elusive *deus ex machina,* the Duke of Florence — than to any of the manoeuvres we actually witness. So how far do we take any or all of these indications to reflect Marston's own view of fate — or, in terms of the Christian faith, the workings of providence? Does our sense of whether the ending of the play presents a harmonious conclusion to an action which has begun (literally!) so inharmoniously depend on our answer to that question? Are we dealing simply with the formal necessities of a tragi-comedy? Or are the questions we should be asking as much to do with the forms and conventions themselves as with the moral dilemmas they appear to frame?

'Pissing against the world'?

In the *Parnassus* plays, staged at Cambridge between 1598 and 1601, the character representing Marston (under his pseudonym of Kinsayder) is censured for 'lifting up your leg and pissing against the world'. And in Ben Jonson's *The Poetaster* the Marston-figure, Crispinus, is given a pill to vomit up his windy words. Is Marston's vision of humankind most aptly expressed in such excremental terms? Are the apparent excesses in which he deals — linguistic and behavioural — his own stylistic mannerisms, or themselves targets for his scorn? Or are they somehow *both,* in a complex manner that is both satiric *and* self-critical? In terms of *The Malcontent* specifically: how far is Malevole keeping his distance from what he censoriously observes, and how far is he concupiscently obsessed by it? Or in asking such questions are we mistakenly trying to deal in biographical and psychological terms with a play that works emblematically?

Modern critics are evenly divided, and what T.S. Eliot wrote in 1934 probably remains true — that whereas there is a 'settled' critical opinion of most of his contemporaries, 'about Marston a wide divergence of opinion is still possible'. According to Alfred Harbage, Marston was a 'coterie dramatist' who had a 'compulsion to degrade', while Samuel Schoenbaum has described him as 'stimulating the jaded tastes of his frivolous and sophisticated aristocratic audiences': Malevole's 'hideous imagination' is also Marston's. Against such arguments, Gustav Cross suggests that Marston's 'over-emphasis and exaggeration . . . need not be taken as evidence of a morbid fascination with his subject': rather, his plays 'are philosophic explorations of the moral philosophy of the stoics'. Paul M. Zell saw Marston's work as distinguished among his contemporaries by its recognition and analysis of the 'problem of the normality of concupiscence'. William Slights found Malevole a 'distasteful parody' of Altofront — from which source, however, is supplied the 'need for spiritual regeneration' which is the play's theme. And Brownell Salomon saw *The Malcontent* as rooted in a Calvinist view of predestination, in which God's providence transcends the moral corruption of the world for which Genoa serves as a microcosm.

I have set out these apparently conflicting conclusions because all nonetheless share an expectation that the play *ought* to be making some sort of definitive moral statement through the words and actions of its characters. But elsewhere in this commentary I have stressed my own feelings (closer to those of such critics as G.K. Hunter and Brian Gibbons) that *The Malcontent* is best viewed as an example of 'metatheatre'. Lionel Abel coined this term to describe plays which are similarly self-referential, or whose characters 'are aware of their own theatricality', and he took *Hamlet* as his first example. In these terms, if Malevole is 'playing the role' of a malcontent, it is not in relation to the somehow more 'real' character of Altofront, but in relation to an audience's critical sense of a theatrical type, and of the nature of the whole play as a fiction.

This is not to rule out the moral dimension: but self-aware theatre tends to work best as *dialectic* rather than demonstration, leaving the business of drawing moral conclusions to the audience. Critics happily accept the challenge to draw such conclusions from a multiplicity of viewpoints — but then tend to submerge the multiplicity by adducing evidence only for their preferred conclusion (a fallacious approach from which *Hamlet* has suffered

a good deal more than *The Malcontent*). If there *is* the moral
confusion that some critics perceive — and condemn — in the play,
then it, too, is being 'presented'. And the shifting status of
Malevole, somewhere between mask and self, is making its own
kind of comment — upon the 'mask' of the malcontent and that of
benevolent duke into which it is transformed, upon the nature of
selfhood in a 'real' social world of masks, and upon the nature and
quality of the theatrical illusion which reflects it.

G.K. Hunter believed that 'one reason why revengeful deaths in
the final scene would be wholly inappropriate' is that 'the emotion
they would exact would shatter the sense of a terrible dream now
analyzed, a terrible truth now capable of being understood'. And
he suggested that 'the relationship of Malevole to Altofront is
finally that of dreamer to analyst, of play to spectator, where the
superior reality of the second term is in every case dependent on
his serving the unifying function that the first requires of him'. In
effect, Altofront finally 'disappears from view', and 'the end of the
play invites us to look back into the play as a completed image
whose ordering is now fully revealed, not to look forward in
imagination at what will happen next'. I find this a highly
stimulating interpretation, which is mistaken only insofar as any
discussion of Malevole and Altofront as 'dreamer and analyst' takes
one dangerously close to the next step of seeing the whole play as a
case study in schizophrenia — a view which may have a kernel of
truth in it, but which ultimately no more reflects the way the play
'works' than does discussing *Hamlet* in terms of the Oedipus
complex.

For a theatrical rather than a psychoanalytic parallel, one might
look at the 'dual personality' of Shen Teh and Shui Ta in Brecht's
The Good Woman of Setzuan, in which the title character adopts
the mask of a more worldly-wise cousin in order to survive in the
'real' world. No more than in *The Malcontent* is it relevant in that
play to ask, 'What happens next?' But Brecht, asking the audience
indeed to 'look back into the play as a completed image', explicitly
requires them to consider ways of resolving the dilemma that
Marston, as it were, leaves hanging in the air. How *can* Shen Teh
survive without Shui Ta? How Altofront without Malevole?
Whether or not one perceives Malevole as 'pissing against the
world', Marston, through the creation of Altofront and all the
dramaturgical and moral questions that raises, must finally be
acquitted of pissing against the audience. Rather, he is challenging
them to make the effort of judgement.

Further reading

Texts of the plays

For further study of *The Malcontent* itself, there are annotated
critical editions by M.L. Wine in the Regents Renaissance Drama
Series (Edward Arnold, 1965); by Bernard Harris in the New
Mermaids series (Ernest Benn, 1967); and by George K. Hunter in
the Revels Plays series (Methuen, 1975). There is no adequate
collected edition of the plays: H. Harvey Wood's edition of *The
Plays of John Marston* in three volumes (Edinburgh: Oliver and
Boyd, 1934-39) is readable but unreliable, and the older three-
volume edition by A.H. Bullen, *The Works of John Marston*
(Bullen, 1887), is now perhaps the more accessible, having been
reprinted by Olm in 1970. There are separate critical editions of
Antonio's Revenge and *The Fawn* in the Revels Plays; of *Antonio
and Mellida, Antonio's Revenge,* and *The Dutch Courtesan* in the
Regents Renaissance Drama Series; of *The Dutch Courtesan* in the
Fountainwell Drama Texts; and of *The Wonder of Women* in the
Renaissance Drama series (New York: Garland, 1979).

Social and theatrical background

Una Ellis-Fermor, *The Jacobean Drama: an Interpretation.* London:
    Methuen, 4th ed., 1958.
Brian Gibbons, *Jacobean City Comedy.* Methuen, 2nd ed., 1980.
Andrew Gurr, *The Shakespearean Stage, 1574-1642.* Cambridge
    University Press, 2nd ed., 1980.
Alfred Harbage, *Shakespeare and the Rival Traditions.* Macmillan,
    1952.
Bridget Gellert Lyons, *Voices of Melancholy: Studies in the
    Literary Treatment of Melancholy in Renaissance England.*
    Routledge, 1971.
Robert Ornstein, *The Moral Vision of Jacobean Tragedy.* University
    of Wisconsin Press, 1960.

Studies of the plays

Morse S. Allen, *The Satire of John Marston.* Ohio State University
    Press, 1920.

Anthony Caputi, *John Marston: Satirist*. Ithaca, N.Y.: Cornell University Press, 1961.

Gustav Cross, 'The Retrograde Genius of John Marston', *Studies in English Literature*, II (1961).

Philip J. Finkelpearl, *John Marston of the Middle Temple: an Elizabethan Dramatist in His Social Setting*. Harvard University Press, 1969.

George L. Geckle, *John Marston's Drama: Themes, Images, Sources*. Fairleigh Dickinson University Press, 1980.

G.K. Hunter, 'English Folly and Italian Vice: the Moral Landscape of John Marston', in John Russell Brown and Bernard Harris, eds., *Jacobean Theatre* (Edward Arnold, 1960).

Reginald W. Ingram, *John Marston*. Boston: Twayne, 1978.

E. Jensen, 'Theme and Imagery in the Malcontent', *Studies in English Literature*, X (1970).

C. Kieffer, 'Music and Marston's *The Malcontent*', *Studies in Philology*, LI (1954).

J.D. Peter, 'John Marston's Plays', *Scrutiny*, XVII (1950).

Samuel Schoenbaum, 'The Precarious Balance of John Marston', *PMLA*, LXXVII (1952); reprinted in R.J. Kaufmann, ed., *Elizabethan Drama* (Oxford University Press, 1961).

Michael Scott, *John Marston's Plays: Theme, Structure, and Performance*. Macmillan, 1978.

Paul M. Zall, 'John Marston, Satirist', *ELH*, XX (1953).

THE MALCONTENT

BENIAMINO IONSONIO
POETÆ
ELEGANTISSIMO
GRAVISSIMO
AMICO
SVO CANDIDO ET CORDATO
IOHANNES MARSTON
MVSARVM ALVMNVS
ASPERAM HANC SVAM THALIAM
D.[*at*] D.[*edicatque*]

TO THE READER

I am an ill orator; and, in truth, use to indite more honestly
than eloquently, for it is my custom to speak as I think, and
write as I speak.

In plainness, therefore, understand that in some things I
have willingly erred, as in supposing a Duke of Genoa, and in 5
taking names different from that city's families; for which
some may wittily accuse me; but my defence shall be as honest
as many reproofs unto me have been most malicious: since, I
heartily protest, it was my care to write so far from reasonable
offence that even strangers in whose state I laid my scene 10
should not from thence draw any disgrace to any, dead or
living. Yet, in despite of my endeavours, I understand some
have been most unadvisedly over-cunning in misinterpreting
me, and with subtlety (as deep as hell) have maliciously spread
ill rumours, which, springing from themselves, might to 15
themselves have heavily returned. Surely I desire to satisfy
every firm spirit, who, in all his actions, proposeth to himself
no more ends than God and virtue do, whose intentions are
always simple; to such I protest that with my free understanding I have not glanced at disgrace of any but of those 20
whose unquiet studies labour innovation, contempt of holy
policy, reverend comely superiority, and established unity.
For the rest of my supposed tartness, I fear not but unto
every worthy mind it will be approved so general and honest
as may modestly pass with the freedom of a satire. I would 25
fain leave the paper; only one thing afflicts me, to think that
scenes invented merely to be spoken should be enforcively
published to be read, and that the least hurt I can receive is to
do myself the wrong. But, since others otherwise would do me
more, the least inconvenience is to be accepted. I have myself 30
therefore set forth this Comedy; but so, that my enforced

3

absence must much rely upon the printer's discretion; but I shall entreat slight errors in orthography may be as slightly over-passed, and that the unhandsome shape which this trifle in reading presents may be pardoned for the pleasure it once   35 afforded you when it was presented with the soul of lively action.

Sine aliqua dementia nullus Phœbus.

I.M.

THE INDUCTION

TO

THE MALCONTENT, AND THE ADDITIONS
ACTED
BY THE KING'S MAJESTY'S SERVANTS.
Written By John Webster.

Enter W. SLY, *a Tire-man following him with a stool.*

Tire. Sir, the gentlemen will be angry if you sit here.

Sly. Why? We may sit upon the stage at the private house.
Thou dost not take me for a country gentleman, dost?
Dost think I fear hissing? I'll hold my life thou tookest
me for one of the players. 5

Tire. No, sir.

Sly. By God's slid, if you had, I would have given you but
sixpence for your stool. Let them that have stale suits sit
in the galleries. Hiss at me! He that will be laughed out
of a tavern or an ordinary shall seldom feed well or be 10
drunk in good company—Where's Harry Condell, Dick
Burbage, and Will Sly? Let me speak with some of
them. [*Sits.*]

Tire. And't please you to go in, sir, you may.

Sly. I tell you, no. I am one that hath seen this play often, 15
and can give them intelligence for their action: I have
most of the jests here in my table-book.

Enter SINKLO.

Sinklo. Save you, coz!

Sly. O, cousin! Come, you shall sit between my legs here.

Sinklo. No, indeed, cousin; the audience then will take me 20
for a viol-de-gambo, and think that you play upon me.

Sly. Nay, rather that I work upon you, coz.

Sinklo. We stayed for you at supper last night at my cousin
Honeymoon's, the woollen-draper. After supper we drew
cuts for a score of apricocks, the longest cut still to draw 25
an apricock: by this light, 'twas Mistress Frank Honeymoon's fortune still to have the longest cut. I did measure
for the women—What be these, coz?

Enter D. BURBAGE, H. CONDELL, *and* J. LOWIN.

Sly. The players!—God save you! [*Stands and bows.*]

Bur. You are very welcome.   30

Sly. I pray you, know this gentleman, my cousin. 'Tis Master
   Doomsday's son, the usurer.

Cond. I beseech you, sir, be covered.

Sly. No, in good faith, for mine ease; look you, my hat's the
   handle to this fan. [*fans himself*] God's so, what a beast   35
   was I, I did not leave my feather at home! Well, but I'll
   take an order with you.   *Puts his feather in his pocket*

Bur. Why do you conceal your feather, sir?

Sly. Why? Do you think I'll have jests broken upon me in
   the play, to be laughed at? This play hath beaten all your   40
   gallants out of the feathers; Blackfriars hath almost
   spoiled Blackfriars for feathers.

Sinklo. God's so, I thought 'twas for somewhat our gentle-
   women at home counselled me to wear my feather to the
   play: yet I am loath to spoil it.   45

Sly. Why, coz?

Sinklo. Because I got it in the tilt-yard. There was a herald
   broke my pate for taking it up; but I have worn it up and
   down the Strand, and met him forty times since, and yet
   he dares not challenge it.   50

Sly. Do you hear, sir, this play is a bitter play?

Cond. Why, sir, 'tis neither satire nor moral, but the mean
   passage of a history; yet there are a sort of discontented
   creatures that bear a stingless envy to great ones, and
   these will wrest the doings of any man to their base   55
   malicious applyment; but should their interpretation
   come to the test, like your marmoset they presently turn
   their teeth to their tail and eat it.

Sly. I will not go so far with you; but I say, any man that
   hath wit may censure—if he sit in the twelve penny   60
   room—and I say again, the play is bitter.

Bur. Sir, you are like a patron that presenting a poor scholar
   to a benefice enjoins him not to rail against anything that
   stands within compass of his patron's folly. Why should

not we enjoy the ancient freedom of poesy? Shall we   65
protest to the ladies that their painting makes them
angels? or to my young gallant that his expense in the
brothel shall gain him reputation? No sir, such vices as
stand not accountable to law should be cured as men heal
tetters, by casting ink upon them. Would you be satisfied   70
in anything else, sir?

Sly. Ay, marry, would I: I would know how you came by this
play.

Cond. Faith, sir, the book was lost; and because 'twas pity so
good a play should be lost, we found it, and play it.   75

Sly. I wonder you would play it, another company having
interest in it.

Cond. Why not Malevole in folio with us, as Jeronimo in
decimo-sexto with them? They taught us a name for our
play: we call it *One for another*.   80

Sly. What are your additions?

Bur. Sooth, not greatly needful; only as your sallet to your
great feast, to entertain a little more time, and to abridge
the not-received custom of music in our theatre. I must   84
leave you, sir.   *Exit.*

Sinklo. Doth he play the Malcontent?

Cond. Yes, sir.

Sinklo. I durst lay four of mine ears, the play is not so well
acted as it hath been.

Cond. O, no, sir, nothing *ad Parmenonis suem*.   90

Low. Have you lost your ears, sir, that you are so prodigal of
laying them?

Sinklo. Why did you ask that, friend?

Low. Marry, sir, because I have heard of a fellow would offer
to lay a hundred-pound wager, that was not worth five   95
baubees; and in this kind you might venture four of your
elbows; yet God defend your coat should have so many!

Sinklo. Nay, truly, I am no great censurer; and yet I might
have been one of the College of Critics once. My cousin
here hath an excellent memory indeed, sir.   100

Sly. Who, I? I'll tell you a strange thing of myself; and I

can tell you, for one that never studied the art of memory
'tis very strange too.

Cond. What's that, sir?

Sly. Why, I'll lay a hundred pound, I'll walk but once down   105
by the Goldsmiths' Row in Cheap, take notice of the
signs, and tell you them with a breath instantly.

Low. 'Tis very strange.

Sly. They begin as the world did, with Adam and Eve.
There's in all just five and fifty. I do use to meditate   110
much when I come to plays too. What do you think
might come into a man's head now, seeing all this
company?

Cond. I know not, sir.

Sly. I have an excellent thought: if some fifty of the Grecians   115
that were crammed in the horse-belly had eaten garlic,
do you not think the Trojans might have smelt out their
knavery?

Cond. Very likely.

Sly. By God, I would they had, for I love Hector horribly.   120

Sinklo. O, but, coz, coz:
    'Great Alexander, when he came to the tomb of Achilles,
    Spake with a big loud voice, O thou thrice blessèd and
        happy!'

Sly. Alexander was an ass to speak so well of a filthy cullion.

Low. Good sir, will you leave the stage? I'll help you to a   125
private room.

Sly. Come, coz, let's take some tobacco.—Have you never a
prologue?

Low. Not any, sir.

Sly. Let me see, I will make one extempore: 130
    Come to them, and fencing of a congey with arms and
    legs, be round with them:
    'Gentlemen, I could wish for the women's sakes you had
    all soft cushions; and, gentlewomen, I could wish that for
    the men's sakes you had all more easy standings.'   135
    What would they wish more but the play now? and that
    they shall have instantly.   [*Exeunt.*]

DRAMATIS PERSONAE

GIOVANNI ALTOFRONTO, *disguised* MALEVOLE, *sometime Duke of Genoa.*

PIETRO JACOMO, *Duke of Genoa.*

MENDOZA, *a minion to the Duchess of* PIETRO JACOMO.

CELSO, *a friend to* ALTOFRONT.   5

BILIOSO, *an old choleric marshal.*

PREPASSO, *a gentleman-usher.*

FERNEZE, *a young courtier, and enamoured on the Duchess.*

FERRARDO, *a minion to* DUKE PIETRO JACOMO.

EQUATO ⎫   10
GUERRINO ⎭ *two courtiers.*

PASSARELLO, *fool to* BILIOSO.

AURELIA, *Duchess to* DUKE PIETRO JACOMO.

MARIA, *Duchess to* DUKE ALTOFRONT.

EMILIA ⎫   15
BIANCA ⎭ *two ladies attending on* AURELIA.

MAQUERELLE, *an old panderess.*

[CAPTAIN of the Genoan Citadel.]

[MERCURY, Presenter of the masque.]

[Presenter of the Prologue.]   20

[Presenter of the Epilogue.]

[Pages, a guard, four halberdiers, one with perfume, suitors etc.]

Prologus

An Imperfect Ode, Being But One Staff, Spoken By The
Prologue

To wrest each hurtless thought to private sense
Is the foul use of ill-bred Impudence;
Immodest censure now grows wild,
All over-running.
Let Innocence be ne'er so chaste,   5
Yet at the last
She is defiled
With too nice-brained cunning.
O you of fairer soul,
Control   10
With an Herculean arm
This harm;
And once teach all old freedom of a pen,
Which still must write of fools, whiles't writes of men.

The Malcontent
Act I

ACTUS PRIMUS, SCENA PRIMA.

The vilest out-of-tune music being heard, enter BILIOSO *and* PREPASSO.

Bil. [*Shouts to the upper level of the stage*] Why, how now? are ye mad? or drunk? or both? or what?

Pre. Are ye building Babylon there?

Bil. Here's a noise in court! you think you are in a tavern, do you not?   5

Pre. You think you are in a brothel-house, do you not? This room is ill-scented.

Enter one with a perfume.

So, perfume, perfume; some upon me, I pray thee. The Duke is upon instant entrance: so, make place there.

[*Exit the one with perfume.*]

SCENA SECUNDA.

Enter the Duke PIETRO, FERRARDO, Count EQUATO, Count CELSO *before, and* GUERRINO.

Pietro. Where breathes that music?

Bil. The discord rather than the music is heard from the Malcontent Malevole's chamber.

Ferr. [*Calling*] Malevole! [*Music stops.*]

Mal. (*Out of his chamber*) Yaugh, god-a'-man, what dost thou   5
there? Duke's Ganymede, Juno's jealous of thy long stockings! shadow of a woman, what wouldst, weasel?

thou lamb a' court, what dost thou bleat for? ah, you
smooth-chinned catamite!

Pietro. Come down, thou ragged cur, and snarl here. I give   10
thy dogged sullenness free liberty; trot about and
bespurtle whom thou pleasest.

Mal. I'll come among you, you goatish-blooded toderers, as
gum into taffeta, to fret, to fret. I'll fall like a sponge into
water, to suck up, to suck up. Howl again. I'll go to   15
church, and come to you.   [*Exit above.*]

Pietro. This Malevole is one of the most prodigious affections
that ever conversed with nature, a man, or rather a
monster, more discontent than Lucifer when he was
thrust out of the presence; his appetite is unsatiable as   20
the grave, as far from any content as from heaven. His
highest delight is to procure others vexation, and therein
he thinks he truly serves heaven; for 'tis his position,
whosoever in this earth can be contented is a slave and
damned; therefore does he afflict all in that to which they   25
are most affected. The elements struggle within him; his
own soul is at variance within herself; his speech is
halter-worthy at all hours. I like him, faith; he gives good
intelligence to my spirit, makes me understand those
weaknesses which others' flattery palliates.—Hark! they   30
sing.

SCENA TERTIA.   *A Song.*
     Enter MALEVOLE *after the Song.*

Pietro. See, he comes. Now shall you hear the extremity of
a malcontent: he is as free as air; he blows over every
man. And, sir, whence come you now?

Mal. From the public place of much dissimulation, the
church.   5

Pietro. What didst there?

Mal. Talk with a usurer; take up at interest.

Pietro. I wonder what religion thou art?

Mal. Of a soldier's religion.

Pietro. And what dost think makes most infidels now?   10

Mal. Sects, sects; I have seen seeming Piety change her robe
so oft, that sure none but some arch-devil can shape her
a petticoat.

Pietro. O, a religious policy!

Mal. But damnation on a politic religion! I am weary; would   15
I were one of the Duke's hounds now!

Pietro. But what's the common news abroad, Malevole?
Thou doggest rumour still?

Mal. Common news? why, common words are, 'God save ye,
fare ye well'; common actions, flattery and cozenage;   20
common things, women and cuckolds. And how does
my little Ferrard? Ah, ye lecherous animal! my little
ferret, he goes sucking up and down the palace into every
hen's nest, like a weasel. And to what dost thou addict
thy time to now, more than to those antique painted   25
drabs that are still affected of young courtiers, Flattery,
Pride, and Venery?

Ferr. I study languages. Who dost think to be the best
linguist of our age?

Mal. Phew! the Devil. Let him possess thee, he'll teach thee   30
to speak all languages most readily and strangely; and
great reason, marry; he's travelled greatly i' the world,
and is everywhere.

Ferr. Save i' th' court.

Mal. Ay, save i' th' court. (*To Bilioso*) And how does my old   35
muck-hill overspread with fresh snow? thou half a man,
half a goat, all a beast. How does thy young wife, old
huddle?

Bil. Out, you improvident rascal! [*Kicks at him.*]

Mal. Do, kick, thou hugely-horned old Duke's ox, good   40
Master Make-please.

Pietro. How dost thou live nowadays, Malevole?

Mal. Why, like the knight Sir Patrick Penlolians, with killing
a' spiders for my lady's monkey.

Pietro. How dost spend the night? I hear thou never sleep'st.   45

Mal. O, no, but dream the most fantastical . . . O heaven! O
fubbery, fubbery!

Pietro. Dream! what dreamest?

Mal. Why, methinks I see that signior pawn his footcloth,
that metreza her plate; this madam takes physic, that   50
t'other monsieur may minister to her; here is a pander
jewelled; there is a fellow in shift of satin this day, that
could not shift a shirt t'other night. Here a Paris supports
that Helen; there's a Lady Guinever bears up that Sir
Lancelot—dreams, dreams, visions, fantasies, chimeras,   55
imaginations, tricks, conceits! (*To Prepasso*) Sir Tristram
Trimtram, come aloft Jack-an-apes with a whim-wham:
here's a Knight of the land of Catito shall play at trap
with any page in Europe, do the sword-dance with any
morris-dancer in Christendom, ride at the ring till the   60
fin of his eyes look as blue as the welkin, and run the
wild goose chase even with Pompey the Huge.

Pietro. You run—

Mal. To the Devil! Now, Signior Guerrino, that thou from
a most pitied prisoner shouldst grow a most loathed   65
flatterer! Alas, poor Celso, thy star's oppressed; thou
art an honest lord; 'tis pity.

Eq. Is't pity?

Mal. Ay, marry is't, philosophical Equato; and 'tis pity that
thou, being so excellent a scholar by art, shouldst be so   70
ridiculous a fool by nature. I have a thing to tell you,
Duke. Bid 'um avaunt, bid 'um avaunt.

Pietro. Leave us, leave us. *Exeunt all saving Pietro and
Malevole.* Now, sir, what is't?

Mal. Duke, thou art a *becco*, a *cornuto*.   75

Pietro. How?

Mal. Thou art a cuckold.

Pietro. Speak; unshell him quick.

Mal. With most tumbler-like nimbleness.

Pietro. Who? by whom? I burst with desire.   80

Mal. Mendoza is the man makes thee a horned beast; Duke,
'tis Mendoza cornutes thee.

Pietro. What conformance? relate; short, short!

Mal. As a lawyer's beard:

> There is an old crone in the court,   85
> Her name is Maquerelle,
> She is my mistress, sooth to say,
> And she doth ever tell me—
> Blirt a' rhyme, blirt a' rhyme: Maquerelle is a cunning
> bawd; I am an honest villain; thy wife is a close drab;   90
> and thou art a notorious cuckold. Farewell, Duke.

Pietro. Stay, stay.

Mal. Dull, dull Duke, can lazy patience make lame revenge?
  O God, for a woman to make a man that which God
  never created, never made!   95

Pietro. What did God never make?

Mal. A cuckold. To be made a thing that's hoodwinked with
  kindness, whilst every rascal fillips his brows; to have a
  coxcomb with egregious horns pinned to a lord's back,
  every page sporting himself with delightful laughter, 100
  whilst he must be the last must know it. Pistols and
  poniards! pistols and poniards!

Pietro. Death and damnation!

Mal. Lightning and thunder!

Pietro. Vengeance and torture!   105

Mal. Catso!

Pietro. O, revenge!

Mal. Nay, to select, among ten thousand fairs,
  A Lady far inferior to the most,
  In fair proportion both of limb and soul;   110
  To take her from austerer check of parents,
  To make her his by most devoutful rites,
  Make her commandress of a better essence
  Than is the gorgeous world, even of a man;
  To hug her with as raised an appetite   115
  As usurers do their delved-up treasury
  (Thinking none tells it but his private self);
  To meet her spirit in a nimble kiss,
  Distilling panting ardour to her heart;
  True to her sheets, nay, diets strong his blood   120
  To give her height of hymeneal sweets,—

Pietro. O God!

Mal. Whilst she lisps, and gives him some court-*quelquechose,*
    Made only to provoke, not satiate:
    And yet even then the thaw of her delight   125
    Flows from lewd heat of apprehension,
    Only from strange imagination's rankness
    That forms the adulterer's presence in her soul,
    And makes her think she clips the foul knave's loins.

Pietro. Affliction to my blood's root!   130

Mal. Nay, think, but think what may proceed of this!
    Adultery is often the mother of incest.

Pietro. Incest?

Mal. Yes, incest. Mark: Mendoza of his wife begets per-
    chance a daughter. Mendoza dies. His son marries this 135
    daughter. Say you? Nay, 'tis frequent, not only probable
    but, no question, often acted, whilst ignorance, fearless
    ignorance, clasps his own seed.

Pietro. Hideous imagination!

Mal. Adultery? why, next to the sin of simony, 'tis the most 140
    horrid transgression under the cope of salvation.

Pietro. Next to simony?

Mal. Ay, next to simony, in which our men in next age shall
    not sin.

Pietro. Not sin? Why?   145

Mal. Because (thanks to some churchmen) our age will leave
    them nothing to sin with. But adultery—O dullness!
    †shue, should exemplary punishment,† that intemperate
    bloods may freeze but to think it. I would damn him and
    all his generation: my own hands should do it; ha! I 150
    would not trust heaven with my vengeance anything.

Pietro. Anything, anything, Malevole! Thou shalt see instantly
    what temper my spirit holds. Farewell; remember I
    forget thee not; farewell.   *Exit* PIETRO.

Mal. Farewell.   155
    Lean thoughtfulness, a sallow meditation,
    Suck thy veins dry, distemperance rob thy sleep!
    The heart's disquiet is revenge most deep:

He that gets blood, the life of flesh but spills,
But he that breaks heart's peace, the dear soul kills.   160
Well, this disguise doth yet afford me that
Which kings do seldom hear or great men use—
Free speech; and though my state's usurped,
Yet this affected strain gives me a tongue
As fetterless as is an emperor's.   165
I may speak foolishly, ay, knavishly,
Always carelessly, yet no one thinks it fashion
To peise my breath; "for he that laughs and strikes
"Is lightly felt, or seldom struck again.
Duke, I'll torment thee; now my just revenge   170
From thee than crown a richer gem shall part:
Beneath God, naught's so dear as a calm heart.

SCENA QUARTA.

Enter CELSO.

Celso. My honoured Lord—
Mal. Peace, speak low; peace! O Celso, constant Lord,
    (Thou to whose faith I only rest discovered,
    Thou, one of full ten millions of men,
    That lovèst virtue only for itself;   5
    Thou in whose hands old Ops may put her soul)
    Behold forever-banished Altofront,
    This Genoa's last year's Duke. O truly noble!
    I wanted those old instruments of state,
    Dissemblance and Suspect: I could not time it, Celso;   10
    My throne stood like a point in midst of a circle,
    To all of equal nearness, bore with none,
    Reigned all alike, so slept in fearless virtue,
    Suspectless, too suspectless; till the crowd
    (Still lickerous of untried novelties),   15
    Impatient with severer government,
    Made strong with Florence, banished Altofront.
Celso. Strong with Florence! ay, thence your mischief rose;
    For when the daughter of the Florentine

Was matched once with this Pietro, now Duke,   20
No stratagem of state untried was left,
Till you of all—
Mal.   Of all was quite bereft;
    Alas, Maria too close prisonèd,
    My true-faithed Duchess, i' the Citadel!
Celso. I'll still adhere: let's mutiny and die.   25
Mal. O, no, climb not a falling tower, Celso;
    'Tis well held desperation, no zeal;
    Hopeless to strive with fate; peace, temporize.
    Hope, hope, that never forsakest the wretched'st man,
    Yet bid'st me live, and lurk in this disguise!   30
    What, play I well the free-breathed discontent?
    Why, man, we are all philosophical monarchs or natural
    fools. Celso, the court's afire; the Duchess's sheets will
    smoke for 't ere it be long; impure Mendoza, that sharp-
    nosed Lord that made the cursed match linked Genoa   35
    with Florence, now broad-horns the Duke, which he now
    knows.
    Discord to malcontents is very manna;
    When the ranks are burst, then scuffle Altofront.
Celso. Ay, but durst?   40
Mal. 'Tis gone; 'tis swallow'd like a mineral:
    Some way 'twill work; phewt, I'll not shrink:
    "He's resolute who can no lower sink.

BILIOSO *entering, Malevole shifteth his speech.*

[*To Celso*] O the father of May-poles! did you never see
a fellow whose strength consisted in his breath, respect   45
in his office, religion on his lord, and love in himself?
why, then, behold.
Bil. Signior—
Mal. My right worshipful lord, your court night-cap makes
    you have a passing high forehead.   50
Bil. I can tell you strange news, but I am sure you know
    them already: the Duke speaks much good of you.

Mal. Go to, then: and shall you and I now enter into a strict
friendship?

Bil. Second one another?   55

Mal. Yes.

Bil. Do one another good offices?

Mal. Just. What though I called thee old ox, egregious
wittol, broken-bellied coward, rotten mummy? yet, since
I am in favour—   60

Bil. Words of course, terms of disport. His grace presents
you by me a chain, as his grateful remembrance for—I
am ignorant for what;—marry, ye may impart—yet
howsoever—come—dear friend—dost know my son?

Mal. Your son?   65

Bil. He shall eat woodcocks, dance jigs, make possets, and
play at shuttlecock with any young lord about the court.
He has as sweet a lady too—dost know her little bitch?

Mal. 'Tis a dog, man.

Bil. Believe me, a she-bitch: O, 'tis a good creature! thou   70
shalt be her servant. I'll make thee acquainted with my
young wife too. What! I keep her not at court for
nothing. 'Tis grown to supper-time; come to my table:
that, anything I have, stands open to thee.

Mal. (*To Celso*) How smooth to him that is in state of grace,   75
How servile, is the rugged'st courtier's face!
What profit, nay, what nature would keep down,
Are heaved to them are minions to a crown.
Envious ambition never sates his thirst,
Till sucking all, he swells and swells, and bursts.   80

Bil. I shall now leave you with my always-best wishes; only
let's hold betwixt us a firm correspondence, a mutual-
friendly-reciprocal kind of steady-unanimous, heartily-
leagued—

Mal. Did your signiorship ne'er see a pigeon-house that was   85
smooth, round, and white without, and full of holes and
stink within? ha' ye not, old courtier?

Bil. O, yes, 'tis the form, the fashion of them all.

Mal. Adieu, my true court-friend; farewell, my dear Castilio.

Exit BILIOSO.

Celso. Yonder's Mendoza.   *Descries Mendoza.*

Mal.   True; the privy-key.   90

Celso. I take my leave, sweet Lord.

Mal.   'Tis fit; away!   *Exit* CELSO.

SCENA QUINTA.

Enter MENDOZA *with three or four* Suitors.

Men. Leave your suits with me; I can and will; attend my
    secretary; leave me.   [*Exeunt* Suitors.]

Mal. Mendoza, hark ye, hark ye. You are a treacherous
    villain: God b' wi' ye!

Men. Out, you base-born rascal!   5

Mal. We are all the sons of heaven, though a tripe-wife were
    our mother. Ah, you whoreson, hot-reined he-marmoset!
    Egistus! didst ever hear of one Egistus?

Men. Gistus?

Mal. Ay, Egistus; he was a filthy incontinent fleshmonger,   10
    such a one as thou art.

Men. Out, grumbling rogue!

Mal. Orestes, beware Orestes!

Men. Out, beggar!

Mal. I once shall rise.   15

Men. Thou rise!

Mal. Ay, at the resurrection.
    "*No vulgar seed but once may rise, and shall;*
    "*No King so huge but 'fore he die, may fall.*   *Exit.*

Men. Now good Elysium! what a delicious heaven is it for a   20
    man to be in a prince's favour! O sweet God! O pleasure!
    O fortune! O all thou best of life! what should I think?
    what say? what do? To be a favourite! a minion! to have
    a general timorous respect observe a man, a stateful
    silence in his presence, solitariness in his absence, a con-   25
    fused hum and busy murmur of obsequious suitors
    training him, the cloth held up and way proclaimed

before him; petitionary vassals licking the pavement with
their slavish knees, whilst some odd palace lamprels that
engender with snakes, and are full of eyes on both sides, 30
with a kind of insinuated humbleness fix all their delights
upon his brow. O blessed state! What a ravishing pros-
pect doth the Olympus of favour yield! Death, I cornute
the Duke! Sweet women, most sweet ladies, nay, angels!
by heaven, he is more accursed than a devil that hates 35
you, or is hated by you; and happier than a god that
loves you, or is beloved by you—you preservers of mankind, life-blood of society. Who would live, nay, who
can live without you? O Paradise! how majestical is your
austerer presence! how imperiously chaste is your more 40
modest face! but, O, how full of ravishing attraction is
your pretty, petulant, languishing, lasciviously-composed
countenance! these amorous smiles, those soul-warming
sparkling glances, ardent as those flames that singed the
world by heedless Phaeton! in body how delicate, in 45
soul how witty, in discourse how pregnant, in life how
wary, in favours how judicious, in day how sociable, and
in night how—O pleasure unutterable! indeed, it is most
certain, one man cannot deserve only to enjoy a beau-
teous woman: but a Duchess! In despite of Phoebus, I'll 50
write a sonnet instantly in praise of her.   *Exit.*

Scena Sexta.

Enter FERNEZE *ushering* AURELIA; EMILIA *and* MAQUERELLE
bearing up her train, BIANCA *attending. All go out but* AURELIA,
MAQUERELLE, *and* FERNEZE.

Aur. And is 't possible? Mendoza slight me! possible?
Fern. Possible!
    What can be strange in him that 's drunk with favour,
    Grows insolent with grace? Speak, Maquerelle, speak.
Maq. To speak feelingly, more, more richly in solid sense 5
    than worthless words, give me those jewels of your ears
    to receive my enforced duty. As for my part, 'tis well

known I can put up anything (*Ferneze privately feeds
Maquerelle's hands with jewels during this speech*), can
bear patiently with any man. But when I heard he   10
wronged your precious sweetness, I was enforced to take
deep offence. 'Tis most certain he loves Emilia with high
appetite; and, as she told me (as you know we women
impart our secrets one to another) when she repulsed his
suit in that he was possessed with your endeared grace   15
Mendoza most ingratefully renounced all faith to you.

Fern. Nay, called you— Speak, Maquerelle, speak!

Maq. By heaven, 'witch', 'dried biscuit'; and contested
blushlessly he loved you but for a spurt, or so.

Fern. For maintenance.   20

Maq. Advancement and regard.

Aur. O villain! O impudent Mendoza!

Maq. Nay, he is the rustiest-jawed, the foulest-mouthed
knave in railing against our sex; he will rail agin'
women—   25

Aur. How? how?

Maq. I am ashamed to speak 't, I.

Aur. I love to hate him; speak.

Maq. Why, when Emilia scorned his base unsteadiness, the
black-throated rascal scolded, and said—   30

Aur. What?

Maq. Troth, 'tis too shameless.

Aur. What said he?

Maq. Why that at four, women were fools; at fourteen,
drabs; at forty, bawds; at fourscore, witches; and a   35
hundred, cats.

Aur. O unlimitable impudency!

Fern. But as for poor Ferneze's fixèd heart,
Was never shadeless meadow drier parched
Under the scorching heat of heaven's dog,   40
Than is my heart with your enforcing eyes.

Maq. A hot simile!

Fern. Your smiles have been my heaven, your frowns my hell:
O, pity, then! Grace should with beauty dwell.

Maq. [*Aside to Ferneze*] Reasonable perfect, by 'r Lady.   45
Aur. I will love thee, be it but in despite
    Of that Mendoza—witch, Ferneze—witch!
    Ferneze, thou art the Duchess' favourite.
    Be faithful, private; but 'tis dangerous.
Fern. "*His love is lifeless that for love fears breath:*   50
    "*The worst that 's due to sin, O would 'twere death!*
Aur. Enjoy my favour. I will be sick instantly and take
    physic; therefore in depth of night visit—
Maq. Visit her chamber, but conditionally you shall not
    offend her bed; by this diamond!   55
Fern. By this diamond—   *Gives it to Maquerelle.*
Maq. Nor tarry longer than you please; by this ruby!
Fern. By this ruby—   *Gives again.*
Maq. And that the door shall not creak.
Fern. And that the door shall not creak.   60
Maq. Nay, but swear.
Fern. By this purse—   *Gives her his purse.*
Maq. Go to, I'll keep your oaths for you. Remember, visit.

        Enter MENDOZA, *reading a sonnet.*

Aur. Dried biscuit!—Look where the base wretch comes.
Men. '*Beauty's life, heaven's model, love's queen,*'—   65
Maq. That 's his Emilia.
Men. '*Nature's triumph, best on earth,*'—
Maq. Meaning Emilia.
Men. '*Thou only wonder that the world hath seen,*'—
Maq. That 's Emilia.   70
Aur. Must I then hear her praised?—Mendoza!
Men. Madam, your excellency is graciously encountered; I
    have been writing passionate flashes in honour of—
                          Exit FERNEZE.
Aur. Out, villain, villain! O judgment, where have been my
    eyes, what bewitched election made me dote on thee,   75
    what sorcery made me love thee? But, begone; bury thy
    head. O that I could do more than loathe thee!
    Hence, worst of ill!

No reason ask, our reason is our will.

Exit with MAQUERELLE.

Men. Women? nay, Furies; nay, worse; for they torment   80
only the bad, but women good and bad.

Damnation of mankind! Breath, hast thou praised them
for this? And is 't you, Ferneze, are wriggled into
smock-grace? Sit sure! O, that I could rail against these
monsters in nature, models of hell, curse of the earth,   85
women that dare attempt anything, and what they
attempt they care not how they accomplish; without all
premeditation or prevention; rash in asking, desperate in
working, impatient in suffering, extreme in desiring,
slaves unto appetite, mistresses in dissembling, only   90
constant in unconstancy, only perfect in counterfeiting:
their words are feigned, their eyes forged, their sighs
dissembled, their looks counterfeit, their hair false, their
given hopes deceitful, their very breath artificial. *Their*
blood is their only god; bad clothes and old age are only the   95
devils they tremble at.

That I could rail now!

SCENA SEPTIMA.

Enter PIETRO, *his sword drawn.*

Pietro. A mischief fill thy throat, thou foul-jawed slave!
Say thy prayers.

Men. I ha' forgot 'um.

Pietro. Thou shalt die.

Men. So shalt thou. I am heart-mad.   5

Pietro. I am horn-mad.

Men. Extreme mad.

Pietro. Monstrously mad.

Men. Why?

Pietro. Why? Thou—thou hast dishonourèd my bed.   10

Men. I? Come, come, sit;

Here's my bare heart to thee, as steady
As is this centre to the glorious world.

And yet, hark, thou art a *cornuto*—but by me?

Pietro. Yes, slave, by thee.   15

Men. Do not, do not with tart and spleenful breath
    Lose him can loose thee. I offend my Duke!
    Bear record, O ye dumb and raw-aired nights,
    How vigilant my sleepless eyes have been
    To watch the traitor! Record, thou spirit of truth,   20
    With what debasement I ha' thrown myself
    To under-offices, only to learn
    The truth, the party, time, the means, the place,
    By whom, and when, and where thou wert disgraced!
    And am I paid with 'slave'? hath my intrusion   25
    To places private and prohibited,
    Only to observe the closer passages,
    Heaven knows, with vows of revelation,
    Made me suspected, made me deemed a villain?
    What rogue hath wronged us?

Pietro.   Mendoza, I may err.   30

Men. Err? 'tis too mild a name: but err and err,
    Run giddy with suspect 'fore through me thou know
    That which most creatures save thyself do know.
    Nay, since my service hath so loathed reject,
    'Fore I'll reveal, shalt find them clipped together.   35

Pietro. Mendoza, thou knowest I am a most plain-breasted
    man.

Men. The fitter to make a cuckold. Would your brows were
    most plain too!

Pietro. Tell me—indeed, I heard thee rail—   40

Men. At women, true; why, what cold phlegm could choose,
    Knowing a Lord so honest, virtuous,
    So boundless-loving, bounteous, fair-shaped, sweet,
    To be contemned, abused, defamed, made cuckold?
    Heart! I hate all women for 't: sweet sheets, wax lights,   45
    antic bedposts, cambric smocks, villainous curtains,
    arras pictures, oiled hinges, and all the tongue-tied lasci-
    vious witnesses of great creatures' wantonness—what
    salvation can you expect?

Pietro. Wilt thou tell me?   50
Men. Why, you may find it yourself; observe, observe.
Pietro. I ha' not the patience: wilt thou deserve me? Tell,
    give it!
Men. Take 't! Why, Ferneze is the man, Ferneze; I'll prove 't;
    this night you shall take him in your sheets; will 't   55
    serve?
Pietro. It will; my bosom 's in some peace. Till night—
Men. What?
Pietro.   Farewell.
Men.   God, how weak a lord are you!
    Why, do you think there is no more but so?
Pietro. Why?   60
Men. Nay, then, will I presume to counsel you:
    It should be thus.
    You, with some guard, upon the sudden
    Break into the Princess' chamber. I stay behind,
    Without the door through which he needs must pass.   65
    Ferneze flies; let him. To me he comes, he's killed
    By me; observe, by me; you follow; I rail,
    And seem to save the body. Duchess comes,
    On whom (respecting her advancèd birth,
    And your fair nature), I know, nay, I do know,   70
    No violence must be used. She comes, I storm,
    I praise, excuse Ferneze, and still maintain
    The Duchess' honour. She for this loves me;
    I honour you, shall know her soul, you mine.
    Then naught shall she contrive in vengeance   75
    (As women are most thoughtful in revenge)
    Of her Ferneze, but you shall sooner know't
    Than she can think't.
               — Thus shall his death come sure,
    Your Duchess brain-caught: so your life secure.
Pietro. It is too well, my bosom and my heart.   80
    "*When nothing helps, cut off the rotten part.*   *Exit.*
Men. "*Who cannot feign friendship, can ne'er produce the
    effects of hatred.* Honest fool Duke, subtle lascivious

Duchess, silly novice Ferneze, I do laugh at ye. My brain
is in labour till it produce mischief, and I feel sudden   85
throes, proofs sensible the issue is at hand.
"*As bears shape young, so I'll form my device,*
"*Which grown proves horrid: vengeance makes men wise.*
                                                    [*Exit.*]

[SCENA VIII].

Enter MALEVOLE *and* PASSARELLO.

Mal. Fool, most happily encountered. Canst sing, fool?

Pass. Yes, I can sing fool, if you'll bear the burden; and I
      can play upon instruments, scurvily, as gentlemen do.
      O, that I had been gelded! I should then have been a fat
      fool for a chamber, a squeaking fool for a tavern, and a   5
      private fool for all the ladies.

Mal. You are in good case since you came to court, fool.
      What, guarded, guarded!

Pass. Yes, faith, even as footmen and bawds wear velvet, not
      for an ornament of honour, but for a badge of drudgery;   10
      for, now the Duke is discontented, I am fain to fool
      him asleep every night.

Mal. What are his griefs?

Pass. He hath sore eyes.

Mal. I never observed so much.   15

Pass. Horrible sore eyes; and so hath every cuckold, for the
      roots of the horns spring in the eyeballs, and that's the
      reason the horn of a cuckold is as tender as his eye, or
      as that growing in the woman's forehead twelve years
      since, that could not endure to be touched. The Duke   20
      hangs down his head like a columbine.

Mal. Passarello, why do great men beg fools?

Pass. As the Welshman stole rushes when there was nothing
      else to filch; only to keep begging in fashion.

Mal. Pooh, thou givest no good reason; thou speakest like a   25
      fool.

Pass. Faith, I utter small fragments, as your knight courts
your city widow with jingling of his gilt spurs, advancing
his bush-coloured beard, and taking tobacco; this is all
the mirror of their knightly compliments. Nay, I shall   30
talk when my tongue is a-going once; 'tis like a citizen
on horseback, evermore in a false gallop.

Mal. And how doth Maquerelle fare nowadays?

Pass. Faith, I was wont to salute her as our English women
are at their first landing in Flushing: I would call her   35
whore; but now that antiquity leaves her as an old piece
of plastic t' work by, I only ask her how her rotten teeth
fare every morning, and so leave her. She was the first
that ever invented perfumed smocks for the gentle-
women and woollen shoes, for fear of creaking, for the   40
visitant. She were an excellent lady, but that her face
peeleth like Muscovy glass.

Mal. And how doth thy old lord, that hath wit enough to be
a flatterer, and conscience enough to be a knave?

Pass. O, excellent: he keeps beside me fifteen jesters to   45
instruct him in the art of fooling; and utters their jests
in private to the Duke and Duchess. He'll lie like to your
Switzer or lawyer; he'll be of any side for most money.

Mal. I am in haste, be brief.

Pass. As your fiddler when he is paid. He'll thrive, I warrant   50
you, while your young courtier stands, like Good Friday
in Lent: men long to see it, because more fatting days
come after it; else he's the leanest and pitifull'st actor in
the whole pageant. Adieu, Malevole.

Mal. [*Aside*] O world most vild, when thy loose vanities,   55
Taught by this fool, do make the fool seem wise!

Pass. You'll know me again, Malevole.

Mal. O, ay, by that velvet.

Pass. Ay, as a pettifogger by his buckram bag. I am as
common in the court as an hostess's lips in the country;   60
knights, and clowns, and knaves, and all share me: the
court cannot possibly be without me. Adieu, Malevole.

[*Exeunt.*]

Act II

Enter MENDOZA *with a sconce to observe* FERNEZE's *entrance who, whilst the act is playing, enter unbraced, two* pages *before him with lights, is met by* MAQUERELLE *and conveyed in. The* pages *are sent away.*

Men. He's caught, the woodcock's head is i' th' noose!
    Now treads Ferneze in dangerous path of lust,
    Swearing his sense is merely deified.
    The fool grasps clouds, and shall beget centaurs;
    And now, in strength of panting faint delight,   5
    The goat bids heaven envy him. Good goose,
    I can afford thee nothing but the poor
    Comfort of calamity, pity.
    "Lust's like the plummets hanging on clock-lines,
    "Will ne'er a' done till all is quite undone;   10
    Such is the course salt sallow lust doth run;
    Which thou shalt try.
    I'll be revenged. Duke, thy suspect, Duchess, thy dis-
    grace, Ferneze, thy rivalship, shall have swift vengeance.
    Nothing so holy, no band of nature so strong, no law of   15
    friendship so sacred, but I'll profane, burst, violate,
    'fore I'll endure disgrace, contempt, and poverty.
    Shall I, whose very 'hum' struck all heads bare,
    Whose face made silence, creaking of whose shoe
    Forced the most private passages fly ope,   20
    Scrape like a servile dog at some latched door?
    Learn now to make a leg, and cry 'Beseech ye,
    Pray ye, is such a Lord within?', be awed
    At some odd usher's scoffed formality?

First sear my brains! *Unde cadis non quo refert*;   25
My heart cries, 'Perish all! How? how?' *What fate*
"Can once avoid revenge, that's desperate?
I'll to the Duke; if all should ope—if! tush,
"Fortune still dotes on those who cannot blush.   [*Exit.*]

SCENA SECUNDA.

Enter MALEVOLE *at one door;* BIANCA, EMILIA, *and*
MAQUERELLE *at the other door.*

Mal. Bless ye, cast a' ladies!—Ha, Dipsas! how dost thou, old
    coal?

Maq. Old coal?

Mal. Ay, old coal. Methinks thou liest like a brand under
    these billets of green wood. He that will inflame a young   5
    wench's heart, let him lay close to her an old coal that
    hath first been fired, a pandress, my half-burnt lint, who
    though thou canst not flame thyself, yet art able to set a
    thousand virgins' tapers afire. (*To Bianca*) And how does
    Janivere thy husband, my little periwinkle? Is 'a troubled   10
    with the cough a' the lungs still? does he hawk a' nights
    still? He will not bite!

Bian. No, by my troth, I took him with his mouth empty of
    old teeth.

Mal. And he took thee with thy belly full of young bones.   15
    Marry, he took his maim by the stroke of his enemy.

Bian. And I mine by the stroke of my friend.

Mal. The close stock! O mortal wench! [*To Maquerelle*]
    Lady, ha' ye now no restoratives for your decayed
    Jasons? Look ye, crab's guts baked, distilled ox-pith,   20
    the pulverized hairs of a lion's upper-lip, jelly of cock-
    sparrows, he-monkey's marrow, or powder of fox-stones?
    And whither are all you ambling now?

Bian. To bed, to bed.

Mal. Do your husbands lie with ye?   25

Bian. That were country fashion, i' faith.

Mal. Ha' ye no foregoers about you? come, whither in good
    deed, la, now?

Maq. In good indeed, la, now, to eat the most miraculously,
    admirably, astonishable-composed posset with three   30
    curds, without any drink. Will ye help me with a he-fox?
    Here's the Duke.   *The* Ladies *go out.*

Mal. (*To Bianca*) Fried frogs are very good, and French-like,
    too.

Scena Tertia.

Enter Duke PIETRO, Count CELSO, Count EQUATO, BILIOSO,
             FERRARDO *and* MENDOZA.

Pietro. The night grows deep and foul; what hour is 't?

Celso. Upon the stroke of twelve.

Mal. Save ye, Duke!

Pietro. From thee. Begone! I do not love thee; let me see thee
    no more; we are displeased.   5

Mal. Why, God b' wi' thee! Heaven hear my curse:
    May thy wife and thee live long together!

Pietro. Begone, sirrah!

Mal. [*Sings*] *When Arthur first in court began,*—Agamemnon
    —Menelaus—*was ever any duke a* cornuto?   10

Pietro. Begone hence!

Mal. What religion wilt thou be of next?

Men. [*To Bilioso*] Out with him!

Mal. [*To Pietro*] With most servile patience. Time will come
    When wonder of thy error will strike dumb   15
    Thy bezzled sense.
      †Slaves I favour, I marry shall he, rise,†
      "*Good God! how subtle hell doth flatter vice!*
      "*Mounts him aloft, and makes him seem to fly,*
      "*As fowl the tortoise mocked, who to the sky*   20
      "*Th' ambitious shell-fish raised! Th' end of all*
      "*Is only that from height he might dead fall.*

Bil. Why, when? out, ye rogue! Begone, ye rascal!

Mal. I shall now leave ye with all my best wishes.

Bil. Out, ye cur!   25
Mal. Only let 's hold together a firm correspondence.
Bil. Out!
Mal. A mutual-friendly-reciprocal-perpetual kind of steady-
    unanimous heartily-leagued—
Bil. Hence, ye gross-jawed peasantly! Out, go!   30
Mal. Adieu, pigeon-house; thou burr that only stickest to
    nappy fortunes. The serpigo, the strangury, an eternal
    uneffectual priapism seize thee!
Bil. Out, rogue!
Mal. May'st thou be a notorious wittolly pander to thine own   35
    wife, and yet get no office, but live to be the utmost
    misery of mankind, a beggarly cuckold!   *Exit.*
Pietro. It shall be so.
Men. It must be so, for where great states revenge,
    "'Tis requisite, the parts with piety   40
    "And loft respect forbears, be closely dogged.
    "Lay one into his breast shall sleep with him,
    "Feed in the same dish, run in self-faction,
    "Who may discover any shape of danger;
    "For once disgraced, displayèd in offence,   45
    "It makes man blushless, and man is (all confess)
    "More prone to vengeance than to gratefulness.
    "Favours are writ in dust; but stripes we feel;
    "Depravèd nature stamps in lasting steel.
Pietro. You shall be leagued with the Duchess.   50
Equato. The plot is very good.
Pietro. You shall both kill, and seem the corse to save.
Ferr. A most fine brain-trick.
Celso. (*Tacitè*)   Of a most cunning knave.
Pietro. My Lords, the heavy action we intend
    Is death and shame, two of the ugliest shapes   55
    That can confound a soul; think, think of it.
    I strike; but yet, like him that 'gainst stone walls
    Directs his shafts, rebounds in his own face,
    My Lady's shame is mine, O God, 'tis mine!
    Therefore I do conjure all secrecy: 60

Let it be as very little as may be; pray ye, as may be.
Make frightless entrance, salute her with soft eyes,
Stain naught with blood; only Ferneze dies,
But not before her brows. O gentlemen,
God knows I love her! Nothing else, but this.   65
I am not well; if grief, that sucks veins dry,
Rivels the skin, casts ashes in men's faces,
Be-dulls the eye, unstrengthens all the blood,
Chance to remove me to another world,
As sure I once must die, let him succeed: [*Pointing to*   70
     Mendoza]
I have no child; all that my youth begot
Hath been your loves, which shall inherit me;
Which as it ever shall, I do conjure it,
Mendoza may succeed. He's noble born;
With me of much desert.   75

Celso. (*Tacitè*) Much!

Pietro. Your silence answers, 'Ay';
I thank you. Come on now. O, that I might die
Before her shame 's displayed! Would I were forced
To burn my father's tomb, unhele his bones,   80
And dash them in the dirt, rather than this!
This both the living and the dead offends:
"*Sharp surgery where naught but death amends.*

Exit with the others.

SCENA QUARTA.

Enter MAQUERELLE, EMILIA, *and* BIANCA, *with the posset.*

Maq. Even here it is, three curds in three regions individually
     distinct; most methodical, according to art, composed
     without any drink.

Bian. Without any drink?

Maq. Upon my honour. Will ye sit and eat?   5

Emil. Good, the composure, the receipt, how is 't?

Maq. 'Tis a pretty pearl; by this pearl, (how does't with me?)
     [*Emilia gives Maquerelle the pearl*] thus it is: seven and

thirty yolks of Barbary hens' eggs; eighteen spoonfuls
and a half of the juice of cock-sparrow bones; one ounce,   10
three drams, four scruples and one quarter of the syrup
of Ethiopian dates; sweetened with three quarters of a
pound of pure candied Indian eringoes; strewed over
with the powder of pearl of America, amber of Cataia,
and lamb-stones of Muscovia.   15

Bian. Trust me, the ingredients are very cordial and, no
question, good and most powerful in restoration.

Maq. I know not what you mean by restoration; but this it
doth: it purifieth the blood, smootheth the skin, en-
liveneth the eye, strengtheneth the veins, mundifieth the   20
teeth, comforteth the stomach, fortifieth the back, and
quickeneth the wit; that 's all.

Emil. By my troth, I have eaten but two spoonfuls, and
methinks I could discourse most swiftly and wittily
already.   25

Maq. Have you the art to seem honest?

Bian. I thank advice and practice.

Maq. Why, then, eat me a' this posset, quicken your blood,
and preserve your beauty. Do you know Doctor Plaster-
face? by this curd, he is the most exquisite in forging of   30
veins, sprightening of eyes, dyeing of hair, sleeking of
skins, blushing of cheeks, surfling of breasts, blanching
and bleaching of teeth, that ever made an old lady
gracious by torchlight; by this curd, la.

Bian. Well, we are resolved; what God has given us we'll   35
cherish.

Maq. Cherish anything saving your husband; keep him not
too high, lest he leap the pale. But, for your beauty, let it
be your saint; bequeath two hours to it every morning in
your closet. I ha' been young, and yet, in my conscience,   40
I am not above five and twenty; but, believe me, preserve
and use your beauty; for youth and beauty once gone,
we are like beehives without honey, out-a-fashion apparel
that no man will wear; therefore use me your beauty.

Emil. Ay, but men say—   45

Maq. Men say! Let men say what the' will. Life a' woman!
　　they are ignorant of your wants. The more in years, the
　　more in perfection the' grow; if they lose youth and
　　beauty, they gain wisdom and discretion; but when our
　　beauty fades, goodnight with us. There cannot be an　50
　　uglier thing to see than an old woman; from which, O
　　pruning, pinching, and painting, deliver all sweet
　　beauties!　　　　　　　　　　　　　　　　[*Music within.*]

Bian. Hark, music!

Maq. Peace, 'tis i' the Duchess' bed-chamber; good rest,　55
　　most prosperously-graced Ladies.

Emil. Good night, sentinel.

Bian. 'Night, dear Maquerelle.

　　　　　　　　　　　　　　Exeunt all but Maquerelle.

Maq. May my posset's operation send you my wit and
　　honesty; and me, your youth and beauty: the pleasingest　60
　　rest!　　　　　　　　　　　　　　　　　　　　*Exit.*

SCENA QUINTA.

A Song

Whilst the song is singing, enter MENDOZA *with his sword drawn,
standing ready to murder Ferneze as he flies from the Duchess's
chamber.*

All. [*Within*] Strike, strike!　　　　　　　　(*Tumult within.*)

Aur. [*Within*] Save my Ferneze! O, save my Ferneze!

Enter FERNEZE *in his shirt, and is received upon Mendoza's sword.*

All. [*Within*] Follow, pursue!

Aur. [*Within*] O, save Ferneze!

Men. Pierce, pierce!

　　　　　　　Thrusts his rapier in Ferneze.

　　　　　　Thou shallow fool, drop there!　　　　5
　　"He that attempts a prince's lawless love
　　"Must have broad hands, close heart, with Argus' eyes,
　　"And back of Hercules, or else he dies.

Enter AURELIA, *Duke* PIETRO, FERRARDO, BILIOSO, CELSO, *and*
                            EQUATO.

All. Follow, follow!

Men. Stand off, forbear, ye most uncivil lords!   10

Pietro. Strike!

> (*Mendoza bestrides the wounded body of Ferneze and seems to
> save him.*)

Men. Do not; tempt not a man resolved:

> Would you, inhuman murderers, more than death?

Aur. O poor Ferneze!

Men. Alas, now all defence too late.

Aur.   He's dead!   15

Pietro. I am sorry for our shame. Go to your bed:

> Weep not too much, but leave some tears to shed
> When I am dead.

Aur. What, weep for thee? my soul no tears shall find.

Pietro. Alas, alas, that women's souls are blind!   20

Men. Betray such beauty! murder such youth! contemn
> civility!

> He loves him not that rails not at him.

Pietro. Thou canst not move us; we have blood enough;

> And please you, lady, we have quite forgot
> All your defects: if not, why, then—

Aur.   Not.

Pietro.   Not.   25

> The best of rest; good night.

>   *Exit* PIETRO *with other* courtiers.

Aur.   Despite go with thee!

Men. Madam, you ha' done me foul disgrace;

> You have wronged him much loves you too much:
> Go to, your soul knows you have.

Aur. I think I have.   30

Men. Do you but think so?

Aur. Nay, sure, I have: my eyes have witnessed thy love.

> Thou hast stood too firm for me—

Men. Why, tell me, fair-cheeked lady, who even in tears

> Art powerfully beauteous, what unadvisèd passion   35

Struck ye into such a violent heat against me?
Speak, what mischief wronged us? what devil injured us?
Speak.

Aur. That thing ne'er worthy of the name of man, Ferneze.
 Ferneze swore thou lovest Emilia;   40
 Which, to advance, with most reproachful breath
 Thou both didst blemish and denounce my love.

Men. Ignoble villain! did I for this bestride
 Thy wounded limbs? for this rank opposite
 Even to my sovereign? for this, O God, for this,   45
 Sunk all my hopes, and with my hopes my life?
 Ripped bare my throat unto the hangman's axe?
 Thou most dishonoured trunk—Emilia! [*Kicks Ferneze.*]
 By life, I know her not—Emilia!
 Did you believe him?

Aur.   Pardon me, I did.   50

Men. Did you? and thereupon you graced him?

Aur. I did.

Men. Took him to favour, nay, even clasped with him?

Aur. Alas, I did.

Men. This night?   55

Aur. This night.

Men. And in your lustful twines the Duke took you?

Aur. A most sad truth.

Men. O God, O God! how we dull honest souls,
 Heavy-brained men, are swallowed in the bogs   60
 Of a deceitful ground, whilst nimble bloods,
 Light-jointed, spirits spent, cut good men's throats,
 And 'scape. Alas, I am too honest for this age,
 Too full of phlegm, and heavy steadiness;
 Stood still whilst this slave cast a noose about me; 65
 Nay, then to stand in honour of him and her,
 Who had even sliced my heart.

Aur. Come, I did err, and am most sorry I did err.

Men. Why, we are both but dead: the Duke hates us;
 "*And those whom Princes do once groundly hate,*   70
 "*Let them provide to die. As sure as fate,*

"*Prevention is the heart of policy.*
Aur. Shall we murder him?
Men. Instantly?
Aur. Instantly, before he casts a plot,   75
    Or further blaze my honour's much-known blot,
    Let's murder him.
Men. I would do much for you; will ye marry me?
Aur. I'll make thee Duke. We are of Medicis;
    Florence our friend; in court my faction   80
    Not meanly strengthful; the Duke then dead;
    We well prepared for change; the multitude
    Irresolutely reeling; we in force;
    Our party seconded; the kingdom mazed;
    No doubt of swift success; all shall be graced.   85
Men. You do confirm me; we are resolute;
    To-morrow look for change; rest confident.
    'Tis now about the immodest waist of night:
    The mother of moist dew with pallid light
    Spreads gloomy shades about the numbèd earth.   90
    Sleep, sleep, whilst we contrive our mischief's birth.
    This man I'll get inhumed. Farewell; to bed.
    Ay, kiss the pillow, dream the Duke is dead.
    So, so, good night.   *Exit* AURELIA.
    How fortune dotes on impudence! I am in private the 95
    adopted son of yon good Prince. I must be Duke. Why,
    if I must, I must. Most silly Lord, name me? O heaven!
    I see God made honest fools to maintain crafty knaves.
    The Duchess is wholly mine too; must kill her husband
    to quit her shame. Much! Then marry her. Ay!   100
    O, I grow proud in prosperous treachery!
    As wrestlers clip, so I'll embrace you all,
    Not to support, but to procure your fall.

Enter MALEVOLE.

Mal. God arrest thee!
Men. At whose suit?   105
Mal. At the devil's. Ha, you treacherous, damnable monster!

How dost? how dost, thou treacherous rogue? Ha, ye
rascal! I am banished the court, sirrah.

Men. Prithee, let's be acquainted; I do love thee, faith.

Mal. At your service, by the Lord, la: shall's go to supper? 110
Let's be once drunk together, and so unite a most vir-
tuously strengthened friendship; shall's, Huguenot,
shall's?

Men. Wilt fall upon my chamber tomorrow morn?

Mal. As a raven to a dunghill. They say there's one dead 115
here; pricked for the pride of the flesh.

Men. Ferneze; there he is; prithee bury him.

Mal. O, most willingly; I mean to turn pure Rochelle churchman, I.

Men. Thou churchman! why, why? 120

Mal. Because I'll live lazily, rail upon authority, deny King's
supremacy in things indifferent, and be a Pope in mine
own parish.

Men. Wherefore dost thou think churches were made?

Mal. To scour plough-shares. I ha' seen oxen plough up 125
altars. *Et nunc seges ubi Sion fuit.*

Men. Strange!

Mal. Nay, monstrous; I ha' seen a sumptuous steeple turned
to a stinking privy; more beastly, the sacredest place
made a dog's kennel; nay, most inhuman, the stoned 130
coffins of long-dead Christians burst up, and made hogs'
troughs: *Hic finis Priami.* Shall I ha' some sack and
cheese at thy chamber? Good night, good mischievous
incarnate devil; good night, Mendoza; ha, ye inhuman
villain, good night, night, fub! 135

Men. Good night. Tomorrow morn?   *Exit* MENDOZA.

Mal. Ay, I will come, friendly Damnation, I will come. I do
descry cross-points; honesty and courtship straddle as
far asunder as a true Frenchman's legs.

Fern. O! 140

Mal. Proclamations! more proclamations!

Fern. O! a surgeon!

Mal. Hark! lust cries for a surgeon. What news from Limbo?

How does the grand cuckold, Lucifer?
Fern. O, help, help! conceal and save me!   145

Ferneze stirs, and Malevole helps him up and conveys him away.

Mal. Thy shame more than thy wounds do grieve me far:
    "Thy wounds but leave upon thy flesh some scar;
    "But fame ne'er heals, still rankles worse and worse;
    "Such is of uncontrollèd lust the curse.
    "Think what it is in lawless sheets to lie;   150
    "But, O Ferneze, what in lust to die!
    "Then, thou that shame respects, O, fly converse
    "With women's eyes and lisping wantonness!
    "Stick candles 'gainst a virgin wall's white back,
    "If they not burn, yet at the least they'll black.   155
    Come, I'll convey thee to a private port,
    Where thou shalt live (O happy man) from court.
    The beauty of the day begins to rise,
    From whose bright form night's heavy shadow flies.
    Now 'gins close plots to work; the scene grows full,   160
    And craves his eyes who hath a solid skull.   *Exeunt.*

Act III

ACTUS TERTIUS. SCENA PRIMA.

Enter PIETRO *the* Duke, MENDOZA, Count EQUATO, *and*
BILIOSO.

Pietro. 'Tis grown to youth of day: how shall we waste this light?
    My heart's more heavy than a tyrant's crown.
    Shall we go hunt? Prepare for field!   *Exit* EQUATO.
Men. Would ye could be merry!
Pietro. Would God I could! Mendoza, bid 'um haste.   5
                        Exit MENDOZA.
    I would fain shift place; O vain relief!

"*Sad souls may well change place, but not change grief:*
As deer, being struck, fly thorough many soils,
Yet still the shaft sticks fast, so—
Bil. A good old simile, my honoured Lord.   10
Pietro. I am not much unlike to some sick man
That long desirèd hurtful drink; at last
Swills in and drinks his last, ending at once
Both life and thirst. O, would I ne'er had known
My own dishonour! Good God, that men should   15
Desire to search out that which, being found, kills all
Their joy of life! to taste the tree of knowledge,
And then be driven from out Paradise!
Canst give me some comfort?

Bil. My Lord, I have some books which have been dedicated   20
to my honour, and I ne'er read 'um, and yet they had
very fine names, *Physic for fortune, Lozenges of sanctified
sincerity*; very pretty works of curates, scriveners, and
schoolmasters. Marry, I remember one Seneca, Lucius
Annaeus Seneca—   25
Pietro. Out upon him! He writ of Temperance and Fortitude,
yet lived like a voluptuous epicure, and died like an
effeminate coward. Haste thee to Florence.
Here, take our letters; see 'um sealed: away!
Report in private to the honoured Duke   30
His daughter's forced disgrace; tell him at length
We know too much; due compliments advance:
"*There's naught that's safe and sweet but ignorance.*

Exit Duke.

Enter BIANCA.

Bil. Madam, I am going Ambassador for Florence; 'twill be
great charges to me.   35
Bian. No matter, my Lord, you have the lease of two manors
come out next Christmas; you may lay your tenants on
the greater rack for it; and when you come home again,
I'll teach you how you shall get two hundred pounds a
year by your teeth.   40

Bil. How, madam?

Bian. Cut off so much from house-keeping: that which is saved by the teeth, you know, is got by the teeth.

Bil. 'Fore God, and so I may; I am in wondrous credit, lady.

Bian. See the use of flattery; I did ever counsel you to flatter   45
greatness, and you have profited well. Any man that will do so shall be sure to be like your Scotch barnacle, now a block, instantly a worm, and presently a great goose; this it is to rot and putrefy in the bosom of greatness.

Bil. Thou art ever my politician! O, how happy is that old   50
lord that hath a politician to his young lady! I'll have fifty gentlemen shall attend upon me; marry, the most of them shall be farmers' sons, because they shall bear their own charges; and they shall go apparelled thus, in sea-water green suits, ash-colour cloaks, watchet stockings,   55
and popinjay-green feathers. Will not the colours do excellent?

Bian. Out upon 't! they'll look like citizens riding to their friends at Whitsuntide, their apparel just so many several parishes.   60

Bil. I'll have it so; and Passarello, my fool, shall go along with me; marry, he shall be in velvet.

Bian. A fool in velvet!

Bil. Ay, 'tis common for your fool to wear satin; I'll have mine in velvet.   65

Bian. What will you wear, then, my Lord?

Bil. Velvet too; marry, it shall be embroidered, because I'll differ from the fool somewhat. I am horribly troubled with the gout. Nothing grieves me but that my doctor hath forbidden me wine, and you know your Ambassador   70
must drink. Didst thou ask thy doctor what was good for the gout?

Bian. Yes; he said, ease, wine, and women, were good for it.

Bil. Nay, thou hast such a wit! what was good to cure it, said he?   75

Bian. Why, the rack. All your empirics could never do the like cure upon the gout the rack did in England, or your

Scotch boot. The French harlequin will instruct you.

Bil. Surely, I do wonder how thou, having for the most part
of thy lifetime been a country body, shouldest have so   80
good a wit.

Bian. Who, I? Why, I have been a courtier thrice two
months.

Bil. So have I this twenty year, and yet there was a gentleman-
usher called me coxcomb t' other day, and to my face too;   85
was't not a backbiting rascal? I would I were better
travelled, that I might have been better acquainted with
the fashions of several countrymen; but my secretary, I
think, he hath sufficiently instructed me.

Bian. How, my Lord?   90

Bil. 'Marry, my good Lord,' quoth he, 'your lordship shall
ever find amongst a hundred Frenchmen, forty hot-shots;
amongst a hundred Spaniards, three-score braggarts;
amongst a hundred Dutchmen, four-score drunkards;
amongst a hundred Englishmen, four-score and ten mad-   95
men; and amongst an hundred Welshmen—'

Bian. What, my Lord?

Bil. 'Four-score and nineteen gentlemen.'

Bian. But since you go about a sad embassy, I would have
you go in black, my Lord.   100

Bil. Why, dost think I cannot mourn unless I wear my hat in
cypress, like an alderman's heir? That's vile, very old,
in faith.

Bian. I'll learn of you shortly; O, we should have a fine
gallant of you, should not I instruct you! How will you   105
bear yourself when you come into the Duke of Florence'
Court?

Bil. Proud enough, and 'twill do well enough. As I walk up
and down the chamber, I'll spit frowns about me, have
a strong perfume in my jerkin, let my beard grow to   110
make me look terrible, salute no man beneath the fourth
button; and 'twill do excellent.

Bian. But there is a very beautiful lady there; how will you
entertain her?

Bil. I'll tell you that when the lady hath entertained me; but 115
to satisfy thee, here comes the fool. Fool, thou shalt
stand for the fair Lady.

Enter PASSARELLO.

Pass. Your fool will stand for your lady most willingly and
most uprightly.

Bil. I'll salute her in Latin.   120

Pass. O, your fool can understand no Latin.

Bil. Ay, but your lady can.

Pass. Why, then, if your lady take down your fool, your fool
will stand no longer for your lady.

Bil. A pestilent fool! 'fore God, I think the world be turned 125
upside down too.

Pass. O, no, sir; for then your lady and all the ladies in the
palace should go with their heels upward, and that were
a strange sight, you know.

Bil. There be many will repine at my preferment.   130

Pass. O, ay, like the envy of an elder sister that hath her
younger made a lady before her.

Bil. The Duke is wondrous discontented.

Pass. Ay, and more melancholic than a usurer having all his
money out at the death of a Prince.   135

Bil. Didst thou see Madam Floria to-day?

Pass. Yes, I found her repairing her face today; the red upon
the white showed as if her cheeks should have been
served in for two dishes of barberries in stewed broth,
and the flesh to them a woodcock.   140

Bil. A bitter fool! Come, madam, this night thou shalt enjoy
me freely, and to-morrow for Florence.

Exit [BIANCA; BILIOSO *retires*].

Pass. What a natural fool is he that would be a pair of boddice
to a woman's petticoat, to be trussed and pointed to
them. Well, I'll 'dog' my lord; and the word is proper; 145
for when I fawn upon him, he feeds me; when I snap
him by the fingers, he spits in my mouth. If a dog's death
were not strangling, I had rather be one than a serving-

man; for the corruption of coin is either the generation 149
of a usurer or a lousy beggar.   [*Exit.*]

SCENA SECUNDA.

Enter MALEVOLE *in some frieze gown, whilst Bilioso reads his
patent.*

Mal. I cannot sleep; my eyes' ill-neighbouring lids
    Will hold no fellowship. O thou pale sober night,
    Thou that in sluggish fumes all sense dost steep,
    Thou that gives all the world full leave to play,
    Unbend'st the feebled veins of sweaty labour—   5
    The galley-slave, that all the toilsome day
    Tugs at his oar against the stubborn wave,
    Straining his rugged veins, snores fast;
    The stooping scythe-man, that doth barb the field,
    Thou makest wink sure. In night all creatures sleep;   10
    Only the malcontent, that 'gainst his fate
    Repines and quarrels—alas, he's goodman tell-clock!
    His sallow jaw-bones sink with wasting moan;
    Whilst others' beds are down, his pillow's stone.
Bil. Malevole!   15
Mal. (*To Bilioso*) Elder of Israel, thou honest defect of
    wicked nature and obstinate ignorance, when did thy
    wife let thee lie with her?
Bil. I am going Ambassador to Florence.
Mal. Ambassador? Now, for thy country's honour, prithee, 20
    do not put up mutton and porridge i' thy cloak-bag. Thy
    young lady wife goes to Florence with thee too, does she
    not?
Bil. No, I leave her at the palace.
Mal. At the palace! Now discretion shield man! for God's 25
    love, let's ha' no more cuckolds! Hymen begins to put
    off his saffron robe; keep thy wife i' the state of grace.
    Heart a' truth, I would sooner leave my lady singled in a
    bordello than in the Genoa palace:
    Sin there appearing in her sluttish shape   30

Would soon grow loathsome, even to blushless sense;
Surfeit would choke intemperate appetite,
Make the soul scent the rotten breath of lust.
When in an Italian lascivious palace, a lady guardianless,
Left to the push of all allurement,   35
The strongest incitements to immodesty—
To have her bound, incensed with wanton sweets,
Her veins filled high with heating delicates,
Soft rest, sweet music, amorous masquerers, lascivious
banquets, sin itself gilt o'er, strong fantasy tricking up   40
strange delights, presenting it dressed pleasingly to sense,
sense leading it unto the soul, confirmed with potent
example, impudent custom, enticed by that great bawd
Opportunity; thus being prepared, clap to her easy ear
youth in good clothes, well-shaped, rich, fair-spoken,   45
promising-noble, ardent, blood-full, witty, flattering,—
Ulysses absent, O Ithaca, can chastest Penelope hold out?

Bil. Mass, I'll think on 't. Farewell.

Mal. Farewell. Take thy wife with thee. Farewell.

Exit BILIOSO.

To Florence, um? it may prove good, it may;   50
And we may once unmask our brows.

SCENA TERTIA.

Enter Count CELSO.

Celso. My honoured Lord—

Mal. Celso, peace! how is 't? speak low; pale fears
Suspect that hedges, walls, and trees, have ears.
Speak, how runs all?

Celso. I' faith, my Lord, that beast with many heads,   5
The staggering multitude, recoils apace:
Though, thorough great men's envy, most men's malice,
Their much intemperate heat hath banished you,
Yet now they find envy and malice ne'er
Produce faint reformation.   10
The Duke, the too soft Duke, lies as a block,

       For which two tugging factions seem to saw;
       But still the iron through the ribs they draw.
Mal. I tell thee, Celso, I have ever found
       Thy breast most far from shifting cowardice   15
       And fearful baseness: therefore I'll tell thee, Celso,
       I find the wind begins to come about;
       I'll shift my suit of fortune.
       I know the Florentine, whose only force,
       By marrying his proud daughter to this prince,   20
       Both banished me and made this weak lord Duke,
       Will now forsake them all; be sure he will.
       I'll lie in ambush for conveniency
       Upon their severance to confirm myself.
Celso. Is Ferneze interred?   25
Mal. Of that at leisure; he lives.
Celso. But how stands Mendoza? how is 't with him?
Mal. Faith, like a pair of snuffers: snibs filth in other men,
       and retains it in himself.
Celso. He does fly from public notice, methinks, as a hare does   30
       from hounds; the feet whereon he flies betrays him.
Mal. I can track him, Celso.
       O, my disguise fools him most powerfully.
       For that I seem a desperate malcontent,
       He fain would clasp with me; he is the true slave   35
       That will put on the most affected grace
       For some vild second cause.
Celso.   He's here.
Mal.   Give place.

                                        CELSO [*retires.*]

                    Enter MENDOZA.

       Illo, ho, ho, ho! art there, old truepenny?
       Where hast thou spent thyself this morning? I see
       flattery in thine eyes and damnation i' thy soul. Ha, ye   40
       huge rascal!
Men. Thou art very merry.
Mal. As a scholar *futuens gratis.* How does the devil go with
       thee now?

Men. Malevole, thou art an arrant knave.   45

Mal. Who, I ? I have been a sergeant, man.

Men. Thou art very poor.

Mal. As Job, an alchemist, or a poet.

Men. The Duke hates thee.

Mal. As Irishmen do bum-cracks.   50

Men. Thou hast lost his amity.

Mal. As pleasing as maids lose their virginity.

Men. Would thou wert of a lusty spirit! would thou wert noble!

Mal. Why, sure, my blood gives me I am noble, sure I am of   55
noble kind; for I find myself possessed with all their
qualities—love dogs, dice, and drabs, scorn wit in stuff-
clothes, have beat my shoemaker, knocked my sempstress, cuckold' my pothecary, and undone my tailor.
Noble, why not? since the Stoic said, *Neminem servum*   60
non ex regibus, neminem regem non ex servis esse oriundum.
Only busy Fortune touses, and the provident chances
blends them together. I'll give you a simile: did you e'er
see a well with two buckets; whilst one comes up full to
be emptied, another goes down empty to be filled? Such   65
is the state of all humanity. Why, look you, I may be the
son of some Duke; for, believe me, intemperate lascivious
bastardy makes nobility doubtful—I have a lusty daring
heart, Mendoza.

Men. Let's grasp; I do like thee infinitely; wilt enact one   70
thing for me?

Mal. Shall I get by it?

                    [*Mendoza*] *gives him his purse.*
            Command me; I am thy slave beyond death and hell.

Men. Murder the Duke!

Mal. My heart's wish, my soul's desire, my fantasy's dream,   75
my blood's longing, the only height of my hopes! How,
O God, how? O, how my united spirits throng together!
So strengthen my resolve!

Men. The Duke is now a-hunting.

Mal. Excellent, admirable, as the devil would have it! Lend   80 me, lend me, rapier, pistol, cross-bow—so, so, I'll do it.

Men. Then we agree.

Mal. As Lent and fishmongers. Come 'a *cap-a-pe?* How in
 form?

Men. Know that this weak-brained Duke, who only stands 85
 on Florence' stilts, hath out of witless zeal made me his
 heir, and secretly confirmed the wreath to me after his
 life's full point.

Mal. Upon what merit?

Men. Merit! by heaven, I horn him! Only Ferneze's death 90
 gave me state's life. Tut, we are politic, he must not live
 now.

Mal. No reason, marry. But how must he die now?

Men. My utmost project is: to murder the Duke that I might
 have his state, because he makes me his heir; to banish 95
 the Duchess, that I might be rid of a cunning Lacedemonian, because I know Florence will forsake her; and
 then to marry Maria, the banished Duke Altofront's wife,
 that her friends might strengthen me and my faction; this
 is all, la. 100

Mal. Do you love Maria?

Men. Faith, no great affection, but as wise men do love great
 women, to ennoble their blood and augment their
 revenue. To accomplish this now, thus now: the Duke is
 in the forest next the sea; single him, kill him, hurl him 105
 i' the main, and proclaim thou sawest wolves eat him.

Mal. Um! not so good. Methinks when he is slain, to get some
 hypocrite, some dangerous wretch that's muffled o'er
 with feigned holiness, to swear he heard the Duke on
 some steep cliff lament his wife's dishonour, and in an 110
 agony of his heart's torture hurled his groaning sides into
 the swollen sea. This circumstance well-made sounds
 probable; and hereupon the Duchess—

Men. May well be banished. O unpeerable invention! rare!
 thou god of policy! it honeys me. 115

Mal. Then fear not for the wife of Altofront; I'll close to her.

Men. Thou shalt, thou shalt. Our excellency is pleased. Why

  wert not thou an emperor? when we are Duke, I'll make
  thee some great man, sure.
Mal. Nay, make me some rich knave, and I'll make myself 120
  some great man.
Men. In thee be all my spirit. Retain ten souls, unite thy
  virtual powers; resolve; ha, remember greatness! Heart,
  farewell.
  "The fate of all my hopes in thee doth dwell. [*Exit.*] 125

     CELSO [*comes forward.*]

Mal. Celso, didst hear? O Heaven, didst hear
  Such devilish mischief? sufferest thou the world
  Carouse damnation even with greedy swallow,
  And still dost wink, still does thy vengeance slumber?
  "If now thy brows are clear, when will they thunder? 130
            Exeunt.

SCENA QUARTA.

 Enter PIETRO, FERRARDO, PREPASSO, *and three* Pages.

Ferr. The dogs are at a fault.   *Cornets like horns.*
Pietro. Would God nothing but the dogs were at it! Let the
  deer pursue safety, the dogs follow the game, and do you
  follow the dogs. As for me, 'tis unfit one beast should
  hunt another; I ha' one chaseth me. And 't please you, I 5
  would be rid of ye a little.
Ferr. Would your grief would as soon leave you as we to
  quietness!
Pietro. I thank you. *Exeunt* [FERRARDO *and* PREPASSO].
  Boy, what dost thou dream of now?   10
First Page. Of a dry summer, my Lord; for here's a hot world
  towards. But, my Lord, I had a strange dream last night.
Pietro. What strange dream?
First Page. Why, methought I pleased you with singing, and
  then I dreamt you gave me that short sword. 15
Pietro. Prettily begged. Hold thee, I'll prove thy dream true;
  take't.   [*Gives sword.*]
First Page. My duty! but still I dreamt on, my Lord; and

methought, and 't shall please your Excellency, you
would needs out of your royal bounty give me that jewel   20
in your hat.

Pietro. O, thou didst but dream, boy; do not believe it;
    dreams prove not always true; they may hold in a short
    sword, but not in a jewel. But now, sir, you dreamt you
    had pleased me with singing; make that true, as I ha'   25
    made the other.

First Page. Faith, my Lord, I did but dream, and dreams,
    you say, prove not always true; they may hold in a good
    sword, but not in a good song: the truth is, I ha' lost my
    voice.   30

Pietro. Lost thy voice; how?

First Page. With dreaming, faith: but here's a couple of
    sirenical rascals shall enchant ye. What shall they sing,
    my good Lord?

Pietro. Sing of the nature of women; and then the song shall   35
    be surely full of variety; old crotchets, and most sweet
    closes. It shall be humorous, grave, fantastic, amorous,
    melancholy, sprightly, one in all, and all in one.

First Page. All in one?

Pietro. By 'r Lady, too many. Sing: my speech grows culp-   40
    able of unthrifty idleness; sing.

Song.

Ah, so, so, sing. I am heavy; walk off; I shall talk in my
sleep; walk off.   *Exeunt* Pages [*the* Duke *sleeps*].

SCENA QUINTA.

Enter MALEVOLE, *with cross-bow and pistol.*

Mal. Brief, brief! Who? the Duke? good heaven, that fools
    should stumble upon greatness! Do not sleep, Duke;
    give ye good morrow; must be brief, Duke; I am feed to
    murder thee. Start not! Mendoza, Mendoza hired me;
    here's his gold, his pistol, cross-bow, sword; 'tis all as   5
    firm as earth. O fool, fool, choked with the common
    maze of easy idiots, credulity! Make him thine heir!
    What, thy sworn murderer!

Pietro. O, can it be?

Mal. Can. 10

Pietro. Discovered he not Ferneze?

Mal. Yes, but why? but why? For love to thee? Much, much!

—To be revenged upon his rival, who had thrust his jaws awry; who being slain (supposed by thine own 15 hands, defended by his sword) made thee most loathsome, him most gracious with thy loose princess. Thou, closely yielding egress and regress to her, madest him heir; whose hot unquiet lust straight toused thy sheets, and now would seize thy state. Politician! wise man! death! 20 to be led to the stake like a bull by the horns; to make even kindness cut a gentle throat! Life! why art thou numbed? thou foggy dulness, speak! Lives not more faith in a home-thrusting tongue than in these fencing tip-tap courtiers? 25

Enter CELSO, *with a hermit's gown and beard.*

Pietro. Lord, Malevole, if this be true—

Mal. If! come, shade thee with this disguise. If! thou shalt handle it; he shall thank thee for killing thyself. Come, follow my directions, and thou shalt see strange sleights.

Pietro. World, whither wilt thou? 30

Mal. Why, to the devil. Come, the morn grows late.

A steady quickness is the soul of state. *Exeunt.*

Act IV

Actus Quartus. Scena Prima.

Enter MAQUERELLE *knocking at the ladies' door.*

Maq. Medam, Medam, are you stirring, Medam? if you be
stirring, Medam—if I thought I should disturb ye—
               [*Enter* Page.]

Page. My Lady is up, forsooth.

Maq. A pretty boy; faith, how old art thou?

Page. I think fourteen.   5

Maq. Nay, and ye be in the teens—are ye a gentleman born?
do you know me? my name is Medam Maquerelle; I lie
in the old Cunny Court.

    See, here, the ladies.   [*Exit* Page.]

Enter BIANCA *and* EMILIA.

Bian. A fair day to ye, Maquerelle.   10

Emil. Is the Duchess up yet, sentinel?

Maq. O ladies, the most abominable mischance! O dear
ladies, the most piteous disaster! Ferneze was taken last
night in the Duchess's chamber. Alas, the Duke catched
him and killed him!   15

Bian. Was he found in bed?

Maq. O, no; but the villainous certainty is, the door was not
bolted, the tongue-tied hatch held his peace; so the naked
troth is he was found in his shirt, whilst I, like an arrant
beast, lay in the outward chamber, heard nothing; and   20
yet they came by me in the dark, and yet I felt them not,
like a senseless creature as I was. O beauties, look to

53

your busk-points, if not chastely, yet charily; be sure
the door be bolted.—Is your Lord gone to Florence?

Bian. Yes, Maquerelle.   25

Maq. I hope you'll find the discretion to purchase a fresh
gown 'fore his return. Now, by my troth, beauties, I
would ha' ye once wise: he loves ye, pish! he is witty,
bubble! fair-proportioned, mew! nobly-born, wind! Let
this be still your fixed position: esteem me every man   30
according to his good gifts, and so ye shall ever remain
'most dear and most worthy to be most dear' ladies.

Emil. Is the Duke returned from hunting yet?

Maq. They say not yet.

Bian. 'Tis now in midst of day.   35

Emil. How bears the Duchess with this blemish now?

Maq. Faith, boldly; strongly defies defame, as one that has a
duke to her father. And there's a note to you: be sure of
a stout friend in a corner, that may always awe your
husband. Mark the 'haviour of the Duchess now: she   40
dares defame; cries, 'Duke, do what thou canst, I'll quite
mine honour'. Nay, as one confirmed in her own virtue
against ten thousand mouths that mutter her disgrace,
she's presently for dances.

Enter FERRARDO.

Bian. For dances!   45

Maq. Most true.

Emil. Most strange. See, here's my servant, young Ferrard.
How many servants think'st thou I have, Maquerelle?

Maq. The more, the merrier. 'Twas well said, use your
servants as you do your smocks; have many, use one, and   50
change often; for that's most sweet and court-like.

Ferr. Save ye, fair ladies, is the Duke returned?

Bian. Sweet sir, no voice of him as yet in Court.

Ferr. 'Tis very strange.

Bian. And how like you my servant, Maquerelle?   55

Maq. I think he could hardly draw Ulysses' bow; but, by my
fidelity, were his nose narrower, his eyes broader, his

hands thinner, his lips thicker, his legs bigger, his feet
lesser, his hair blacker, and his teeth whiter, he were a
tolerable sweet youth, i' faith. And he will come to my   60
chamber, I will read him the fortune of his beard.

Cornets sound.

Ferr. Not yet returned; I fear—but the Duchess approacheth.

SCENA SECUNDA.

Enter MENDOZA *supporting the* Duchess [AURELIA], GUERRINO;
the Ladies that are on the stage rise; FERRARDO *ushers in the*
Duchess, *and then takes a lady to tread a measure* [*Music sounds*].

Aur. We will dance—music!—we will dance.
Guer. Les quanto, lady, *Pensez bien, Passa regis,* or *Bianca's
    brawl?*
Aur. We have forgot the brawl.
Ferr. So soon? 'tis wonder.   5
Guer. Why? 'tis but two singles on the left, two on the right,
    three doubles forward, a traverse of six round; do this
    twice, three singles side, galliard trick of twenty,
    coranto-pace; a figure of eight, three singles broken
    down, come up, meet, two doubles, fall back, and then   10
    honour.
Aur. O Daedalus, thy maze! I have quite forgot it.
Maq. Trust me, so have I, saving the falling-back, and then
    honour.

Enter PREPASSO.

Aur. Music, music!   15
Pre. Who saw the Duke? the Duke?
Aur. Music!

Enter EQUATO.

Eq. The Duke? Is the Duke returned?
Aur. Music!

Enter CELSO.

Celso. The Duke is either quite invisible, or else is not.   20

Aur. We are not pleased with your intrusion upon our private
retirement; we are not pleased; you have forgot your-
selves.

Enter a Page.

Celso. Boy, thy master? Where's the Duke?

Page. Alas, I left him burying the earth with his spread joy-   25
less limbs. He told me he was heavy, would sleep; bid me
walk off, for that the strength of fantasy oft made him talk
in his dreams. I straight obeyed, nor ever saw him since;
but wheresoe'er he is, he's sad.

Aur. Music, sound high, as is our heart, sound high!   30

SCENA TERTIA.

Enter MALEVOLE, *and* PIETRO *disguised like an hermit.*

Mal. The Duke—peace! [*The music stops.*]—the Duke is
dead.

Aur. Music!

Mal. Is't music?

Men. Give proof.   5

Ferr. How?

Celso. Where?

Pre. When?

Mal. Rest in peace, as the Duke does; quietly sit; for my own
part, I beheld him but dead; that's all. Marry, here's   10
one can give you a more particular account of him.

Men. Speak, holy father, nor let any brow
Within this presence fright thee from the truth.
Speak confidently and freely.

Aur. We attend.   15

Pietro. Now had the mounting sun's all-ripening wings
Swept the cold sweat of night from earth's dank breast,
When I, whom men call Hermit of the Rock,
Forsook my cell, and clambered up a cliff,
Against whose base the heady Neptune dashed   20
His high-curled brows; there 'twas I eased my limbs,
When, lo! my entrails melted with the moan

Someone, who far 'bove me was climbed, did make—
I shall offend.

Men. Not.   25

Aur. On.

Pietro. Methinks I hear him yet: 'O female faith!
   Go sow the ingrateful sand, and love a woman!
   And do I live to be the scoff of men?
   To be the wittol-cuckold, even to hug   30
   My poison? Thou knowest, O truth!
   Sooner hard steel will melt with southern wind,
   A seaman's whistle calm the ocean,
   A town on fire be extinct with tears,
   Than women, vowed to blushless impudence,   35
   With sweet behaviour and soft minioning
   Will turn from that where appetite is fixed.
   O powerful blood, how thou dost slave their soul!
   I washed an Ethiop, who, for recompense,
   Sullied my name. And must I then be forced   40
   To walk, to live thus black? Must! must! fie!
   He that can bear with "must", he cannot die.'
   With that, he sighed too passionately deep,
   That the dull air even groaned. At last he cries,
   'Sink shame in seas, sink deep enough!' so dies.   45
   For then I viewed his body fall, and souse
   Into the foamy main. O, then I saw
   That which methinks I see; it was the Duke;
   Whom straight the nicer-stomached sea belched up.
   But then—   50

Mal. Then came I in; but, 'las, all was too late!
   For even straight he sunk.

Pietro. Such was the Duke's sad fate.

Celso. A better fortune to our Duke Mendoza!

Omnes. Mendoza!   *Cornets flourish.*

Men. A guard, a guard!

Enter a Guard.

We, full of hearty tears,   56

For our good father's loss
(For so we well may call him
Who did beseech your loves for our succession),
Cannot so lightly over-jump his death   60
As leave his woes revengeless. (*To Aurelia*) Woman of
    shame,
We banish thee for ever to the place
From whence this good man comes; nor permit, on
    death,
Unto the body any ornament;
But, base as was thy life, depart away.   65

Aur. Ungrateful—

Men. Away!

Aur. Villain, hear me!

> PREPASSO *and* GUERRINO *lead away the Duchess.*

Men. Begone!

My Lords, address to public council;
'Tis most fit.   70
The train of Fortune is borne up by wit.
Away! our presence shall be sudden; haste.

> *All depart, saving Mendoza, Malevole and Pietro.*

Mal. Now, you egregious devil! ha, ye murdering politician!
how dost, Duke? how dost look now? brave Duke, i'
faith!   75

Men. How did you kill him?

Mal. Slatted his brains out, then soused him in the briny sea.

Men. Brained him, and drowned him too?

Mal. O 'twas best, sure work;
For he that strikes a great man, let him strike home, or else 80
'ware, he'll prove no man. Shoulder not a huge fellow, unless
you may be sure to lay him in the kennel.

Men. A most sound brain-pan! I'll make you both emperors.

Mal. Make us Christians, make us Christians.

Men. I'll hoist ye, ye shall mount.   85

Mal. To the gallows, say ye? come: *praemium incertum petit
certum scelus.* How stands the progress?

Men. Here, take my ring unto the citadel;
    Have entrance to Maria, the grave duchess
    Of banished Altofront. Tell her we love her;   90
    Omit no circumstance to grace our person. Do 't.
Mal. I'll make an excellent pander. Duke, farewell; due
    adieu, Duke.
Men. Take Maquerelle with thee; for 'tis found
    None cuts a diamond but a diamond.   *Exit* MALEVOLE.
    Hermit, thou art a man for me, my confessor;   96
    O thou selected spirit, born for my good,
    Sure thou wouldst make an excellent Elder
    In a deformed church. Come,
    We must be inward, thou and I all one.   100
Pietro. I am glad I was ordained for ye.
Men. Go to then; thou must know that Malevole is a strange
    villain; dangerous, very dangerous. You see how broad 'a
    speaks; a gross-jawed rogue. I would have thee poison
    him; he's like a corn upon my great toe, I cannot go for 105
    him; he must be cored out, he must. Wilt do 't, ha?
Pietro. Anything, anything.
Men. Heart of my life! thus then to the citadel:
    Thou shalt consort with this Malevole;
    There being at supper, poison him: 110
    It shall be laid upon Maria, who yields love or dies.
    Scud quick.
Pietro. Like lightning. "*Good deeds crawl, but mischief flies.*
                                   Exit PIETRO.

Enter MALEVOLE.

Mal. Your devilship's ring has no virtue. The buff-captain,
    the sallow Westphalian gammon-faced zaza cries, 'Stand 115
    out'; must have a stiffer warrant, or no pass into the
    Castle of Comfort.
Men. Command our sudden letter—Not enter? sha't! what
    place is there in Genoa but thou shalt? into my heart, into
    my very heart. Come, let's love; we must love, we two, 120
    soul and body.

Mal. How didst like the hermit? a strange hermit, sirrah.

Men. A dangerous fellow, very perilous; he must die.

Mal. Ay, he must die.

Men. Thou'st kill him. We are wise; we must be wise.   125

Mal. And provident.

Men. Yea, provident. Beware an hypocrite;
  A churchman once corrupted, O, avoid!
  A fellow that makes religion his stalking-horse,
                              (*Shoots under his belly*)
  He breeds a plague: thou shalt poison him.   130

Mal. Ho, 'tis wondrous necessary. How?

Men. You both go jointly to the citadel;
  There sup, there poison him; and Maria,
  Because she is our opposite, shall bear
  The sad suspect; on which she dies, or loves us.   135

Mal. I run.   *Exit* MALEVOLE.

Men. *We that are great, our sole self-good still moves us.*
  They shall die both, for their deserts craves more
  Than we can recompense; their presence still
  Imbraids our fortunes with beholdingness,   140
  Which we abhor; like deed, not doer. Then conclude,
  They live not to cry out ingratitude.
  One stick burns t' other, steel cuts steel alone.
  'Tis good trust few; but, O, 'tis best trust none!
                              Exit MENDOZA.

SCENA QUARTA.

Enter MALEVOLE *and* PIETRO *still disguised, at several doors.*

Mal. How do you? how dost, Duke?

Pietro. O let the last day fall, drop, drop on our cursed heads!
  Let heaven unclasp itself, vomit forth flames!

Mal. O do not rand, do not turn player; there's more of them
  than can well live one by another already. What, art an   5
  infidel still?

Pietro. I am amazed; struck in a swoon with wonder. I am commanded to poison thee.

Mal. I am commanded to poison thee—at supper.

Pietro. At supper!   10

Mal. In the citadel.

Pietro. In the citadel!

Mal. Cross capers, tricks! Truth a' heaven! he would discharge us as boys do eldern guns, one pellet to strike out another. Of what faith art now?   15

Pietro. All is damnation, wickedness extreme; there is no faith in man.

Mal. In none but usurers and brokers; they deceive no man: men take 'um for blood-suckers, and so they are. Now, God deliver me from my friends!   20

Pietro. Thy friends?

Mal. Yes, from my friends; for from mine enemies I'll deliver myself. O, cut-throat friendship is the rankest villainy! Mark this Mendoza; mark him for a villain: but heaven will send a plague upon him for a rogue.   25

Pietro. O world!

Mal. World! 'tis the only region of death, the greatest shop of the devil, the cruellest prison of men, out of the which none pass without paying their dearest breath for a fee; there's nothing perfect in it but extreme, extreme   30 calamity, such as comes yonder.

Scena Quinta.

Enter AURELIA, *two halberts before and two after, supported by* CELSO *and* FERRARDO; AURELIA *in base mourning attire.*

Aur. To banishment! lead on to banishment!

Pietro. Lady, the blessedness of repentance to you!

Aur. Why? why? I can desire nothing but death, nor deserve anything but hell.

 If heaven should give sufficiency of grace   5
 To clear my soul, it would make heaven graceless;
 My sins would make the stock of mercy poor;
 O, they would tire heaven's goodness to reclaim them!

Judgment is just yet from that vast villain;
But, sure, he shall not miss sad punishment   10
'Fore he shall rule. On to my cell of shame!

Pietro. My cell 'tis, lady; where, instead of masks,
Music, tilts, tourneys, and such courtlike shows,
The hollow murmur of the checkless winds
Shall groan again, whilst the unquiet sea   15
Shakes the whole rock with foamy battery.
There usherless the air comes in and out;
The rheumy vault will force your eyes to weep,
Whilst you behold true desolation.
A rocky barrenness shall pierce your eyes,   20
Where all at once one reaches, where he stands,
With brows the roof, both walls with both his hands.

Aur. It is too good. Blessed spirit of my lord,
O, in what orb soe'er thy soul is throned,
Behold me worthily most miserable;   25
O, let the anguish of my contrite spirit
Entreat some reconciliation.
If not, O joy triumph in my just grief;
Death is the end of woes and tears' relief.

Pietro. Belike your lord not loved you, was unkind.   30
Aur. O heaven!
As the soul loved the body, so loved he;
'Twas death to him to part my presence,
Heaven to see me pleased.
Yet I, like to a wretch given o'er to hell,   35
Brake all the sacred rites of marriage,
To clip a base ungentle faithless villain,
O God! a very pagan reprobate—
What should I say?—ungrateful, throws me out,
For whom I lost soul, body, fame, and honour.   40
But 'tis most fit. Why should a better fate
Attend on any who forsake chaste sheets,
Fly the embrace of a devoted heart,
Joined by a solemn vow 'fore God and man,
To taste the brackish blood of beastly lust   45

In an adulterous touch? O ravenous immodesty!
Insatiate impudence of appetite!
Look, here 's your end; for mark, what sap in dust,
What sin in good, even so much love in lust.
Joy to thy ghost, sweet lord, pardon to me!   50

Celso. 'Tis the Duke's pleasure this night you rest in court.

Aur. Soul, lurk in shades; run, shame, from brightsome skies:
In night the blind man misseth not his eyes.

Exit [with CELSO, FERRARDO, *and halberts].*

Mal. Do not weep, kind cuckold; take comfort, man; thy
betters have been *beccos*: Agamemnon, Emperor of all   55
the merry Greeks that tickled all the true Troyans, was a
cornuto; Prince Arthur, that cut off twelve kings' beards,
was a *cornuto*; Hercules, whose back bore up heaven,
and got forty wenches with child in one night—

Pietro. Nay, 'twas fifty.   60

Mal. Faith, forty's enow, a' conscience—yet was a *cornuto*.
Patience; mischief grows proud; be wise.

Pietro. Thou pinchest too deep, art too keen upon me.

Mal. Tut, a pitiful surgeon makes a dangerous sore: I'll tent
thee to the ground. Thinkest I'll sustain myself by   65
flattering thee, because thou art a prince? I had rather
follow a drunkard, and live by licking up his vomit, than
by servile flattery.

Pietro. Yet great men ha' done 't.

Mal. Great slaves—fear better than love, born naturally for a   70
coal-basket; though the common usher of princes' presence, Fortune, ha' blindly given them better place. I am
vowed to be thy affliction.

Pietro. Prithee, be;
I love much misery, and be thou son to me.   75

Mal. Because you are an usurping duke—

Enter BILIOSO.

(*To Bilioso*) Your lordship 's well returned from Florence.

Bil. Well returned, I praise my horse.

Mal. What news from the Florentines?

Bil. I will conceal the Great Duke's pleasure; only this was 80
    his charge: his pleasure is, that his daughter die, Duke
    Pietro be banished for banishing his blood's dishonour,
    and that Duke Altofront be re-accepted. This is all. But
    I hear Duke Pietro is dead.

Mal. Ay, and Mendoza is Duke; what will you do? 85

Bil. Is Mendoza strongest?

Mal. Yet he is.

Bil. Then yet I'll hold with him.

Mal. But if that Altofront should turn straight again?

Bil. Why, then, I would turn straight again. 90
    'Tis good run still with him that has most might:
    I had rather stand with wrong, than fall with right.

Mal. What religion will you be of now?

Bil. Of the Duke's religion, when I know what it is.

Mal. O Hercules! 95

Bil. Hercules? Hercules was the son of Jupiter and Alcmena.

Mal. Your Lordship is a very wittol.

Bil. Wittol?

Mal. Ay, all-wit.

Bil. Amphitryo was a cuckold. 100

Mal. Your lordship sweats; your young lady will get you a
    cloth for your old worship's brows.   *Exit* BILIOSO.
    Here's a fellow to be damned: this is his inviolable
    maxim—'flatter the greatest and oppress the least': a
    whoreson flesh-fly, that still gnaws upon the lean galled 105
    backs.

Pietro. Why dost then salute him?

Mal. Faith, as bawds go to church, for fashion sake. Come,
    be not confounded; th'art but in danger to lose a dukedom.
    Think this—this earth is the only grave and Golgotha 110
    wherein all things that live must rot; 'tis but the draught
    wherein the heavenly bodies discharge their corruption;
    the very muck-hill on which the sublunary orbs cast
    their excrements. Man is the slime of this dung-pit, and
    princes are the governors of these men; for, for our souls, 115
    they are as free as emperors', all of one piece; there goes

but a pair of shears betwixt an emperor and the son of a
bagpiper; only the dyeing, dressing, pressing, glossing,
makes the difference. Now, what art thou like to lose?
A jailer's office to keep men in bonds,   120
Whilst toil and treason all life's good confounds.

Pietro. I here renounce forever regency.

O Altofront, I wrong thee to supplant thy right,
To trip thy heels up with a devilish sleight.
For which I now from throne am thrown, world-tricks
  abjure;   125
For vengeance though 't comes slow, yet it comes sure.
O, I am changed; for here, 'fore the dread power,
In true contrition I do dedicate
My breath to solitary holiness,
My lips to prayer; and my breast's care shall be,   130
Restoring Altofront to regency.

Mal. Thy vows are heard, and we accept thy faith.

Undisguiseth himself.

Enter FERNEZE *and* CELSO.

Altofront, Ferneze, Celso, Pietro—
Banish amazement. Come, we four must stand
Full shock of Fortune; be not so wonder-stricken.   135

Pietro. Doth Ferneze live?

Fern.   For your pardon.

Pietro. Pardon and love. Give leave to recollect
My thoughts dispersed in wild astonishment.
My vows stand fixed in heaven, and from hence
I crave all love and pardon.   140

Mal. Who doubts of Providence that sees this change?
A hearty faith to all!
He needs must rise who can no lower fall;
For still impetuous vicissitude
Touseth the world. Then let no maze intrude   145
Upon your spirits; wonder not I rise;
For who can sink that close can temporize?
The time grows ripe for action; I'll detect

My privat'st plot, lest ignorance fear suspect.
Let's close to counsel, leave the rest to fate: 150
Mature discretion is the life of state.   *Exeunt.*

Act V

ACTUS QUINTUS. SCENA PRIMA.

Enter BILIOSO *and* PASSARELLO.

Bil. Fool, how dost thou like my calf in a long stocking?
Pass. An excellent calf, my Lord.
Bil. This calf hath been a reveller this twenty year. When
Monsieur Gundi lay here ambassador, I could have
carried a lady up and down at arm's end in a platter;   5
and I can tell you, there were those at that time who, to
try the strength of a man's back and his arm, would be
coistered. I have measured calves with most of the
palace, and they come nothing near me; besides, I think
there be not many armours in the arsenal will fit me,   10
especially for the headpiece. I'll tell thee—
Pass. What, my Lord?
Bil. I can eat stewed broth as it comes seething off the fire;
or a custard as it comes reeking out of the oven; and I
think there are not many lords can do it. [*Sniffs at his*   15
pomander.] A good pomander, a little decayed in the
scent; but six grains of musk, ground with rose-water,
and tempered with a little civet, shall fetch her again
presently.
Pass. O, ay, as a bawd with aqua-vitae.   20
Bil. And, what, dost thou rail upon the ladies as thou wert
wont?
Pass. I were better roast a live cat, and might do it with more
safety. I am as secret to thieves as their painting. There's
Maquerelle, oldest bawd and a perpetual beggar; did you   25

never hear of her trick to be known in the city?

Bil. Never.

Pass. Why, she gets all the picture-makers to draw her
picture; when they have done, she most courtly finds
fault with them one after another, and never fetcheth   30
them; they, in revenge of this, execute her in pictures as
they do in Germany, and hang her in their shops. By
this means is she better known to the stinkards than if
she had been five times carted.

Bil. 'Fore God, an excellent policy.   35

Pass. Are there any revels to-night, my lord?

Bil. Yes.

Pass. Good my Lord, give me leave to break a fellow's pate
that hath abused me.

Bil. Whose pate?   40

Pass. Young Ferrard, my Lord.

Bil. Take heed, he 's very valiant; I have known him fight
eight quarrels in five days, believe it.

Pass. O, is he so great a quarreller? why, then, he 's an arrant
coward.   45

Bil. How prove you that?

Pass. Why, thus. He that quarrels seeks to fight; and he that
seeks to fight seeks to die; and he that seeks to die seeks
never to fight more; and he that will quarrel, and seeks
means never to answer a man more, I think he 's a   50
coward.

Bil. Thou canst prove anything.

Pass. Anything but a rich knave; for I can flatter no man.

Bil. Well, be not drunk, good fool; I shall see you anon in
the presence.   *Exeunt.*

Scena [II]

Enter MALEVOLE *and* MAQUERELLE, *at several doors opposite,*
singing.

Mal. The Dutchman for a drunkard,

Maq. The Dane for golden locks,

Mal. The Irishman for usquebaugh,

Maq. The Frenchman for the (   ).

Mal. O, thou art a blessed creature! Had I a modest woman   5
to conceal, I would put her to thy custody; for no
reasonable creature would ever suspect her to be in thy
company. Ha, thou art a melodious Maquerelle, thou
picture of a woman and substance of a beast.

Enter PASSARELLO.

Maq. O fool, will ye be ready anon to go with me to the   10
revels? The hall will be so pestered anon.

Pass. Ay, as the country is with attorneys.

Mal. What hast thou there, fool?

Pass. Wine. I have learned to drink since I went with my
lord ambassador; I'll drink to the health of Madam   15
Maquerelle.

Mal. Why? Thou wast wont to rail upon her.

Pass. Ay; but since, I borrowed money of her. I'll drink to
her health now, as gentlemen visit brokers, or as knights
send venison to the City, either to take up more money,   20
or to procure longer forbearance.

Mal. Give me the bowl. I drink a health to Altofront, our
deposed Duke. [*Drinks.*]

Pass. I'll take it so. [*Takes back bowl, and drinks.*] Now I'll
begin a health to Madam Maquerelle. [*Drinks.*]   25

Mal. Pooh! I will not pledge her.

Pass. Why, I pledged your Lord.

Mal. I care not.

Pass. Not pledge Madam Maquerelle! why, then, will I spew
up your lord again with this fool's finger.   30

Mal. Hold; I'll take it. [*Takes bowl, and drinks.*]

Maq. [*To Malevole*] Now thou hast drunk my health. Fool,
I am friends with thee.

Pass. Art? art?

When Griffon saw the reconcilèd quean   35
  Offering about his neck her arms to cast,
He threw off sword and heart's malignant stream,

And lovely her below the loins embraced.—

Adieu, Madam Maquerelle.   *Exit* PASSARELLO.

Mal. And how dost thou think a' this transformation of state   40
now?

Maq. Verily, very well; for we women always note the falling
of the one is the rising of the other; some must be fat,
some must be lean; some must be fools, and some must
be lords; some must be knaves, and some must be   45
officers; some must be beggars, some must be knights;
some must be cuckolds, and some must be citizens. As
for example, I have two court-dogs, the most fawning
curs, the one called Watch, th' other Catch. Now I, like
Lady Fortune, sometimes love this dog, sometimes raise   50
that dog, sometimes favour Watch, most commonly fancy
Catch. Now that dog which I favour I feed; and he 's so
ravenous that what I give he never chaws it, gulps it
down whole without any relish of what he has, but with
a greedy expectation of what he shall have. The other   55
dog now—

Mal. No more dog, sweet Maquerelle, no more dog. And
what hope hast thou of the Duchess Maria? will she
stoop to the Duke's lure? will she come, thinkst?

Maq. Let me see, where's the sign now? ha' ye e'er a   60
calendar? where's the sign, trow you?

Mal. Sign? why, is there any moment in that?

Maq. O, believe me, a most secret power. Look ye, a
Chaldean or an Assyrian, I am sure 'twas a most sweet
Jew, told me, 'court any woman in the right sign, you   65
shall not miss'. But you must take her in the right vein
then; as, when the sign is in Pisces, a fishmonger's wife
is very sociable; in Cancer, a precisian's wife is very
flexible; in Capricorn, a merchant's wife hardly holds
out; in Libra, a lawyer's wife is very tractable, especially   70
if her husband be at the term; only in Scorpio 'tis very
dangerous meddling. Has the Duke sent any jewel, any
rich stones?

Enter Captain.

Mal. Ay, I think those are the best signs to take a lady in.— 75
By your favour, signior, I must discourse with the Lady
Maria, Altofront's Duchess; I must enter for the Duke.

Cap. She here shall give you interview. I received the guard-
ship of this citadel from the good Altofront, and for his
use I'll keep 't, till I am of no use.

Mal. Wilt thou? [*Aside*] O, heavens, that a Christian should 80
be found in a buff-jerkin! Captain Conscience, I love
thee Captain. [*Aloud*] We attend.   *Exit* Captain.
And what hope hast thou of this Duchess's easiness?

Maq. 'Twill go hard; she was a cold creature ever; she hated
monkeys, fools, jesters, and gentlemen-ushers extremely. 85
She had the vild trick on 't, not only to be truly modestly
honourable in her own conscience, but she would avoid
the least wanton carriage that might incur suspect; as,
God bless me, she had almost brought bed-pressing out
of fashion; I could scarce get a fine for the lease of a 90
lady's favour once in a fortnight.

Mal. Now, in the name of immodesty, how many maiden-
heads hast thou brought to the block?

Maq. Let me see—Heaven forgive us our misdeeds—here's
the Duchess.   95

SCENA [III]

Enter MARIA *and* Captain.

Mal. God bless thee, Lady.

Maria. Out of thy company.

Mal. We have brought thee tender of a husband.

Maria. I hope I have one already.

Maq. Nay, by mine honour, Madam, as good ha' ne'er a 5
husband as a banished husband; he 's in another world
now. I'll tell ye, lady, I have heard of a sect that main-
tained, when the husband was asleep the wife might
lawfully entertain another man; for then her husband
was as dead; much more when he is banished.   10

Maria. Unhonest creature!

Maq. Pish, honesty is but an art to seem so. Pray ye, what 's
     honesty, what 's constancy, but fables feigned, odd old
     fools' chat, devised by jealous fools to wrong our liberty?

Mal. Mully, he that loves thee is a duke, Mendoza. He will   15
     maintain thee royally, love thee ardently, defend thee
     powerfully, marry thee sumptuously, and keep thee, in
     despite of Rosicleer or Donzel del Phœbo. There's
     jewels: if thou wilt, so [*Offers jewels: Maria does not
     move*]; if not, so. [*Takes them away.*]   20

Maria. Captain, for God's love, save poor wretchedness
     From tyranny of lustful insolence!
     Enforce me in the deepest dungeon dwell,
     Rather than here; here round about is hell.
     O my dear'st Altofront, where'er thou breathe,   25
     Let my soul sink into the shades beneath,
     Before I stain thine honour; this thou hast:
     And long as I can die, I will live chaste.

Mal. 'Gainst him that can enforce how vain is strife!

Maria. She that can be enforced has ne'er a knife.   30
     She that through force her limbs with lust enrolls,
     Wants Cleopatra's asps and Portia's coals.
     God amend you!   *Exit with* Captain.

Mal. Now, the fear of the devil forever go with thee!
     Maquerelle, I tell thee, I have found an honest woman.   35
     Faith, I perceive, when all is done, there is of women, as
     of all other things, some good, most bad; some saints,
     some sinners. For as nowadays no courtier but has his
     mistress, no captain but has his cockatrice, no cuckold
     but has his horns, and no fool but has his feather; even   40
     so, no woman but has her weakness and feather too, no
     sex but has his—I can hunt the letter no further—
     [*Aside*] O God, how loathsome this toying is to me!
     That a duke should be forced to fool it! Well, *stultorum*
     plena sunt omnia: better play the fool lord than be the   45
     fool lord.—Now, where's your sleights, Madam
     Maquerelle?

Maq. Why, are ye ignorant that 'tis said a squeamish affected

niceness is natural to women; and that the excuse of their
yielding is only, forsooth, the difficult obtaining? You   50
must put her to 't; women are flax, and will fire in a
moment.

Mal. Why, was the flax put into thy mouth, and yet thou—
thou set fire—thou inflame her?

Maq. Marry, but I'll tell ye now, you were too hot.   55

Mal. The fitter to have inflamed the flaxwoman.

Maq. You were too boisterous, spleeny, for, indeed—

Mal. Go, go, thou art a weak pandress; now I see,
  Sooner earth's fire heaven itself shall waste
  Than all with heat can melt a mind that 's chaste.   60
  Go, thou, the Duke's lime-twig! I'll make the Duke
  turn thee out of thine office. What, not get one touch
  of hope, and had her at such advantage!

Maq. Now, a' my conscience, now I think in my discretion,
  we did not take her in the right sign; the blood was not   65
  in the true vein, sure.   *Exit.*

Enter BILIOSO.

Bil. Make way there! the Duke returns from the enthrone-
  ment. Malevole—

Mal. Out, rogue!

Bil. Malevole—   70

Mal. 'Hence, ye gross-jawed peasantly—out, go!'

Bil. Nay, sweet Malevole, since my return I hear you are
  become the thing I always prophesied would be, an
  advanced virtue, a worthily-employed faithfulness, a
  man a' grace, dear friend. Come; what? *Si quoties*   75
  peccant homines . . . if as often as courtiers play the
  knaves, honest men should be angry—Why, look ye,
  we must collogue sometimes, forswear sometimes.

Mal. Be damned sometimes.

Bil. Right; *nemo omnibus horis sapit*, no man can be honest at   80
  all hours; necessity often depraves virtue.

Mal. I will commend thee to the Duke.

Bil. Do; let us be friends, man.

Mal. And knaves, man.

Bil. Right; let us prosper and purchase; our lordships shall   85
live, and our knavery be forgotten.

Mal. He that by any ways gets riches, his means never shames
him.

Bil. True.

Mal. For impudency and faithlessness are the mainstays to   90
greatness.

Bil. By the Lord, thou art a profound lad.

Mal. By the Lord, thou art a perfect knave. Out, ye ancient
Damnation!

Bil. Peace, peace! and thou wilt not be a friend to me as I   95
am a knave, be not a knave to me as I am thy friend,
and disclose me. Peace, cornets!

SCENA [IV]

Enter PREPASSO *and* FERRARDO, *two pages with lights,* CELSO
and EQUATO, MENDOZA *in Duke's robes, and* GUERRINO.

Men. On, on; leave us, leave us. *Exeunt all saving Malevole* [*and
Mendoza*]. Stay, where is the hermit?

Mal. With Duke Pietro, with Duke Pietro.

Men. Is he dead? is he poisoned?

Mal. Dead as the Duke is.   5

Men. Good, excellent; he will not blab. Secureness lives in
secrecy. Come hither, come hither.

Mal. Thou hast a certain strong villainous scent about thee
my nature cannot endure.

Men. Scent, man? What returns Maria, what answer to our   10
suit?

Mal. Cold, frosty. She is obstinate.

Men. Then she's but dead; 'tis resolute she dies;
Black deed only through black deed safely flies.

Mal. Pooh! *Per scelera semper sceleribus tutum est iter.*   15

Men. What! Art a scholar? Art a politician? Sure thou art
an arrant knave.

Mal. Who, I? I have been twice an undersheriff, man.

Men. Hast been with Maria?

Mal. As your scrivener to your usurer I have dealt about   20
    taking of this commodity; but she's cold, frosty. Well, I
    will go rail upon some great man that I may purchase the
    bastinado, or else go marry some rich Genoan lady and
    instantly go travel.

Men. Travel when thou art married?   25

Mal. Ay, 'tis your young lord's fashion to do so, though he
    was so lazy being a bachelor that he would never travel
    so far as the University; yet when he married her, tails
    off, and *catso*, for England!

Men. And why for England?   30

Mal. Because there is no brothel-houses there.

Men. Nor courtesans?

Mal. Neither; your whore went down with the stews, [*Aside*]
    and your punk came up with your puritan.

Men. Canst thou empoison? Canst thou empoison?   35

Mal. Excellently; no Jew, pothecary or politician better.
    Look ye, here's a box—whom wouldst thou empoison?
    —Here's a box, which, opened and the fume ta'en up in
    conduits thorough which the brain purges itself, doth
    instantly for twelve hours' space bind up all show of life   40
    in a deep senseless sleep. Here's another, which, being
    opened under the sleeper's nose, chokes all the power of
    life, kills him suddenly.

Men. I'll try experiments; 'tis good not to be deceived.—
    So, so; catso!   *Seems to poison Malevole.*
    Who would fear that may destroy?
       Death hath no teeth or tongue;
    And he that 's great, to him are slaves
       Shame, murder, fame, and wrong.—
    Celso!   50

Enter CELSO.

Celso. My honoured Lord?

Men. The good Malevole, that plain-tongued man,
    Alas, is dead on sudden, wondrous strangely.

He held in our esteem good place.
Celso, see him buried, see him buried.   55
Celso. I shall observe ye.
Men. And, Celso, prithee, let it be thy care to-night
To have some pretty show, to solemnize
Our high instalment; some music, maskery.
We'll give fair entertain unto Maria,   60
The duchess to the banished Altofront:
Thou shalt conduct her from the citadel
Unto the palace. Think on some maskery.
Celso. Of what shape, sweet Lord?
Men. What shape? Why, any quick-done fiction;   65
As some brave spirits of the Genoan Dukes,
To come out of Elysium, forsooth,
Led in by Mercury, to gratulate
Our happy fortune; some such anything;
Some far-fet trick, good for ladies, some stale toy or
    other,   70
No matter, so 't be of our devising.
Do thou prepare 't; 'tis but for a fashion sake;
Fear not, it shall be graced, man, it shall take.
Celso. All service.
Men. All thanks; our hand shall not be close to thee; farewell.   75
                                    [CELSO *retires.*]

Now is my treachery secure, nor can we fall;
Mischief that prospers, men do virtue call.
I'll trust no man: he that by tricks gets wreaths
Keeps them with steel; no man securely breathes
Out of deserved ranks; the crowd will mutter, 'fool';   80
Who cannot bear with spite, he cannot rule.
The chiefest secret for a man of state
Is to live senseless of a strengthless hate.   *Exit* MENDOZA.
Mal. (*Starts up and speaks*) Death of the damned thief! I'll
make one i' the mask; thou shalt ha' some brave spirits of   85
the antique Dukes.
Celso. [*Comes forward*] My Lord, what strange delusion?
Mal. Most happy, dear Celso; poisoned with an empty box!

I'll give thee all, anon. My lady comes to court; there is
a whirl of fate comes tumbling on; the castle's captain   90
stands for me, the people pray for me, and the Great
Leader of the just stands for me: then courage, Celso!
For no disastrous chance can ever move him
That leaveth nothing but a God above him.   *Exeunt.*

SCENA [V]

> *Enter* PREPASSO *and* BILIOSO, *two* pages *before them;*
> MAQUERELLE, BIANCA, *and* EMILIA.

Bil. Make room there, room for the ladies! why, gentlemen,
will not ye suffer the ladies to be entered in the great
chamber? Why, gallants! And you, sir, to drop your
torch where the beauties must sit too!

Pre. And there's a great fellow plays the knave; why dost   5
not strike him?

Bil. Let him play the knave, a' God's name. Thinkst thou I
have no more wit than to strike a great fellow?—The
music! more lights! revelling scaffolds! do you hear?
Let there be oaths enow ready at the door, swear out   10
the devil himself. Let's leave the ladies, and go see if
the lords be ready for them.   *All save the Ladies depart.*

Maq. And, by my troth, beauties, why do you not put you
into the fashion? This is a stale cut; you must come in
fashion. Look ye, you must be all felt, felt and feather,   15
a felt upon your bare hair. Look ye, these tiring things
are justly out of request now. And, do ye hear, you must
wear falling-bands, you must come into the falling
fashion; there is such a deal a' pinning these ruffs, when
the fine clean fall is worth all; and again, if you should   20
chance to take a nap in the afternoon, your falling-band
requires no poting-stick to recover his form. Believe me,
no fashion to the falling, I say.

Bian. And is not Signior St. Andrew Jaques a gallant fellow
now?   25

Maq. By my maidenhead, la, honour and he agrees as well

     together as a satin suit and woollen stockings.

Emil. But is not Marshal Make-room, my servant in rever-
     sion, a proper gentleman?

Maq. Yes, in reversion, as he had his office; as, in truth, he   30
     hath all things in reversion: he has his mistress in rever-
     sion, his clothes in reversion, his wit in reversion; and,
     indeed, is a suitor to me for my dog in reversion. But,
     in good verity, la, he is as proper a gentleman in reversion
     as—and, indeed, as fine a man as may be, having a red   35
     beard and a pair of warped legs.

Bian. But, i' faith, I am most monstrously in love with Count
     Quidlibet in Quodlibet; is he not a pretty, dapper,
     unidle gallant?

Maq. He is even one of the most busy-fingered lords; he will   40
     put the beauties to the squeak most hideously.

               [*Enter* BILIOSO.]

Bil. Room! make a lane there! the Duke is entering; stand
     handsomely! For beauty's sake, take up the Ladies
     there! So, cornets, cornets!

Scena [VI]

Enter PREPASSO, *joins to* BILIOSO; *two* pages *and lights*,
FERRARDO, MENDOZA; *at the other door, two* pages *with lights*,
and the Captain *leading in* MARIA; *the* Duke *meets* MARIA *and
closeth with her; the rest fall back.*

Men. Madam, with gentle ear receive my suit;
     A kingdom's safety should o'er-peise slight rites;
     Marriage is merely Nature's policy.
     Then since, unless our royal beds be joined,
     Danger and civil tumult frights the state,   5
     Be wise as you are fair, give way to fate.

Maria. What wouldst thou, thou affliction to our house?
     Thou ever devil, 'twas thou that banishedst
     My truly noble lord!

Men. I?   10

Maria. Ay, by thy plots, by thy black stratagems.
    Twelve moons have suffered change since I beheld
    The lovèd presence of my dearest Lord.
    O thou far worse than Death! he parts but soul
    From a weak body; but thou soul from soul   15
    Disseverest, that which God's own hand did knit—
    Thou scant of honour, full of devilish wit!
Men. Well, check your too-intemperate lavishness I can, and
    will.
Maria. What canst?   20
Men. Go to! in banishment thy husband dies.
Maria. *He ever is at home that 's ever wise.*
Men. You'st never meet more; reason should love control.
Maria. Not meet?
    She that dear loves, her love's still in her soul.   25
Men. You are but a woman, lady; you must yield.
Maria. O, save me, thou innated bashfulness,
    Thou only ornament of woman's modesty!
Men. Modesty? death, I'll torment thee.
Maria. Do, urge all torments, all afflictions try;   30
    I'll die my lord's as long as I can die.
Men. Thou obstinate, thou shalt die. Captain,
    That lady's life is forfeited to justice;
    We have examined her, and we do find
    She hath empoisonèd the reverend hermit;   35
    Therefore we command severest custody.
    Nay, if you'll do's no good, you'st do's no harm;
    A tyrant's peace is blood.
Maria. O, thou art merciful; O gracious devil,
    Rather by much let me condemnèd be   40
    For seeming murder, than be damned for thee!
    I'll mourn no more; come, girt my brows with flowers;
    Revel and dance, soul, now thy wish thou hast;
    Die like a bride, poor heart, thou shalt die chaste.

        Enter AURELIA *in mourning habit.*

Aur. *Life is a frost of cold felicity,*   45

And death the thaw of all our vanity.
Was't not an honest priest that wrote so?
Men. Who let her in?
Bil. Forbear.
Pre. Forbear.   50
Aur. Alas, calamity is everywhere.
   Sad misery, despite your double doors,
   Will enter even in court.
Bil. Peace!
Aur. I ha' done; one word: 'take heed'. I ha' done.   55

Enter Mercury with loud music.

Mer. Cyllenian Mercury, the god of ghosts,
   From gloomy shades that spread the lower coasts,
   Calls four high-famèd Genoan Dukes to come,
   And make this presence their Elysium,
   To pass away this high triumphal night   60
   With song and dances, court's more soft delight.
Aur. Are you god of ghosts? I have a suit depending in hell
   betwixt me and my conscience; I would fain have thee
   help me to an advocate.
Bil. Mercury shall be your lawyer, lady.   65
Aur. Nay, faith, Mercury has too good a face to be a right
   lawyer.
Pre. Peace, forbear! Mercury presents the mask.

Cornets: the song to the cornets, which playing, the mask enters:
MALEVOLE, PIETRO, FERNEZE, *and* CELSO, *in white robes,*
with dukes' crowns upon laurel wreaths; pistolets and short swords
under their robes.

Men. Celso, Celso, court Maria for our love.
   Lady, be gracious, yet grace.   70

(Malevole takes his wife to dance.)

Maria. With me, sir?
Mal.   Yes, more lovèd than my breath;
   With you I'll dance.

Maria.   Why then you dance with death.
          But come, sir; I was ne'er more apt to mirth.
          Death gives eternity a glorious breath;
          O, to die honoured, who would fear to die?   75
Mal. They die in fear who live in villainy.
Men. Yes, believe him, lady, and be ruled by him.

          (*Pietro takes his wife Aurelia to dance.*)

Pietro. Madam, with me?
Aur.   Wouldst then be miserable?
Pietro. I need not wish.
Aur. O yet forbear my hand! away! fly! fly!   80
          O seek not her that only seeks to die!
Pietro. Poor lovèd soul!
Aur.   What, wouldst court misery?
Pietro. Yes.
Aur.   She'll come too soon. O my grieved heart!
Pietro. Lady, ha' done, ha' done.
          Come, let's dance; be once from sorrow free.   85
Aur. Art a sad man?
Pietro.   Yes, sweet.
Aur.   Then we'll agree.

Ferneze takes Maquerelle, and Celso, Bianca; then the cornets sound
          the measure, one change, and rest.

Fern. (*To Bianca*) Believe it, lady; shall I swear? let me enjoy
          you in private, and I'll marry you, by my soul.
Bian. I had rather you would swear by your body; I think
          that would prove the more regarded oath with you.   90
Fern. I'll swear by them both, to please you.
Bian. O, damn them not both to please me, for God's sake!
Fern. Faith, sweet creature, let me enjoy you to-night, and
          I'll marry you to-morrow fortnight, by my troth, la.
Maq. 'On his troth, la' believe him not; that kind of cony-   95
          catching is as stale as Sir Oliver Anchovy's perfumed
          jerkin. Promise of matrimony by a young gallant, to
          bring a virgin lady into a fool's paradise, make her a

great woman, and then cast her off—'tis as common as
natural to a courtier, as jealousy to a citizen, gluttony   100
to a puritan, wisdom to an alderman, pride to a tailor,
or an empty hand-basket to one of these sixpenny
damnations. 'Of his troth, la'! Believe him not; traps to
catch pole-cats!

Mal (*To Maria*) Keep your face constant; let no sudden
passion   105
Speak in your eyes.

Maria.   O my Altofront!

Pietro. (*To Aurelia*) A tyrant's jealousies are very nimble;
You receive it all?

Aur. (*To Pietro*) My heart, though not my knees, doth humbly
fall
Low as the earth to thee.   110

Mal. Peace. Next change. No words.

Maria. Speech to such, ay, O, what will affords!

Cornets sound the measure over again; which danced, they unmask.

Men. Malevole!

They environ Mendoza, bending their pistols on him.

Mal. No.

Men. Altofront! Duke Pietro! Ferneze! Ha!   115

All. Duke Altofront! Duke Altofront!   *Cornets, a flourish.*

Men. Are we surprised? What strange delusions mock
Our senses? Do I dream? or have I dreamt
This two days' space? Where am I?

They seize upon Mendoza.

Mal. Where an arch-villain is.   120

Men. O lend me breath till I am fit to die.
For peace with heaven, for your own soul's sake,
Vouchsafe me life.

Pietro. Ignoble villain, whom neither heaven nor hell,
Goodness of God or man, could once make good!   125

Mal. Base treacherous wretch, what grace canst thou expect,

That hast grown impudent in gracelessness?

Men. O, life!

Mal. Slave, take thy life.

    Wert thou defencèd, through blood and wounds,   130
    The sternest horror of a civil fight,
    Would I achieve thee; but prostrate at my feet,
    I scorn to hurt thee: 'tis the heart of slaves
    That deigns to triumph over peasants' graves;
    For such thou art, (*To Pietro and Aurelia*) *since birth doth*
        ne'er enroll   135
    A man 'mong monarchs, but a glorious soul.
    O, I have seen strange accidents of state:
    The flatterer, like the ivy, clip the oak,
    And waste it to the heart; lust so confirmed,
    That the black act of sin itself not shamed   140
    To be termed courtship.
    O, they that are as great as be their sins,
    Let them remember that th' inconstant people
    Love many princes merely for their faces
    And outward shows; and they do covet more   145
    To have a sight of these than of their virtues.
    Yet thus much let the great ones still conceit
    When they observe not Heaven's imposed conditions,
    They are no kings, but forfeit their commissions.

Maq. O good my Lord, I have lived in the court this twenty 150
year; they that have been old courtiers, and come to live
in the city, they are spited at, and thrust to the walls like
apricocks, good my Lord.

Bil. My Lord, I did know your lordship in this disguise; you
heard me ever say, if Altofront did return, I would 155
stand for him. Besides, 'twas your lordship's pleasure to
call me wittol and cuckold: you must not think, but that
I knew you, I would have put it up so patiently.

Mal. [*To the courtiers*] You o'er-joyed spirits, wipe your long-
wet eyes.

    (*Kicks out Mendoza*) Hence with this man: an eagle takes
not flies.   160

(*To Pietro and Aurelia*) You to your vows; (*To
Maquerelle*) and thou unto the suburbs.
(*To Bilioso*) You to my worst friend I would hardly give;
Thou art a perfect old knave. All-pleased live
(*To Celso and the* Captain) You two unto my breast;
(*To Maria*)   thou to my heart.
The rest of idle actors idly part.   165
And as for me, I here assume my right,
To which I hope all's pleased. To all, good night.
                    Cornets, a flourish. Exeunt omnes.

Epilogus

Your modest silence, full of heedy stillness,
Makes me thus speak: a voluntary illness
Is merely 'scuseless, but unwilling error,
Such as proceeds from too rash youthful fervour,
May well be called a fault, but not a sin: 5
Rivers take names from founts where they begin.
    Then let not too severe an eye peruse
The slighter breaks of our reformèd Muse,
Who could herself herself of faults detect,
But that she knows 'tis easy to correct,   10
Though some men's labour. Troth, to err is fit,
As long as wisdom 's not professed, but wit.
Then till another's happier Muse appears,
Till his Thalia feast your learnèd ears,
To whose desertful lamps pleased Fates impart   15
Art above Nature, Judgement above Art,
    Receive this piece, which hope nor fear yet daunteth;
    He that knows most knows most how much he wanteth.

FINIS

Notes

These notes are intended for use by overseas students as well as by English-born readers. The numbers refer to lines within each scene, and not to pages. The abbreviation 'sd' indicates a stage direction.

Dedication
John Marston, disciple of the muses, gives and dedicates this, his harsh comedy, to Benjamin Jonson, most refined and serious of poets, his candid and sincere friend.

To The Reader
1	*orator*	— advocate, one who pleads a case
1	*indite*	— compose, write
7	*wittily*	— knowingly
10	*strangers*	— foreigners (ie, Genoese)
11	*draw*	— infer, deduce
19	*free*	— unprejudiced
21	*labour innovation*	— instigate rebellion, try to change the state of things as they are
22	*reverend comely superiority*	— legitimate authority
25	*modestly*	— moderately
26	*fain leave the paper*	— gladly stop writing
27	*merely*	— entirely, only
29	*do myself the wrong*	— be personally responsible for the publication
30	*least*	— lesser
31	*but so*	— in such a way
33	*slightly*	— inattentively, lightly
38	*Sine aliqua . . . Phoebus*	— no poet is without some madness

The Induction
For further discussion of the Induction, see Commentary, p. xxiv.

    John Webster — playwright and collaborator, author of *The White Devil* and *The Duchess of Malfi*

sd   *Tire-man* — property and wardrobe man

1   *gentlemen* — audience

2 *private house* — the Blackfriars Theatre (see further Commentary, p. viii)

3, 4 *dost* — do, do you

4 *fear hissing* — taunts of the 'groundlings' (the audience standing around the stage of the Globe Theatre)

7 *slid* — eyelid

8 *stale suits* — out of fashion

10 *ordinary* — eating house

14 *go in* — ie, backstage, into the tiring house (changing-room for actors)

16 *intelligence . . . action* — advice regarding their performances

17 *table book* — pocket notebook

18 *coz* — cousin, friend

21 *viol-de-gambo* — an early violoncello

22 *work* — in an obscene sense

23 *stayed* — waited

24- *drew cuts* — drew straws in a lottery
25

25 *apricocks* — apricots

25, *still* — always
27

27 *the longest cut* — an obscene innuendo

32 *usurer* — one who lends money at interest

33 *be covered* — put your hat on

35, *God's so* — a version of 'catso' (see below, I, iii, 106)
43

37 *take an order* — make an arrangement

40- *This play . . . feathers* — the play was first performed at
42 Blackfriars, the centre of the feather industry which suffered because of its mockery of feather-wearing

43 *somewhat* — some purpose

47 *tilt-yard* — the tilting ground in Whitehall where courtly combatants jousted and lost the plumes from their helmets

47 *herald* — one who controlled the tilts

48 *pate* — head

49 *the Strand* — fashionable thoroughfare in London

52- *mean passage* — (i) half-way between (ii) merely a history
53

54 *stingless* — harmless

56 *applyment* — application, interpretation

57 *marmoset* — monkey

60- *twelve-penny room* — an expensive 'box' adjoining the stage
61
63 *benefice* — church living, a financial favour
66 *painting* — make-up
70 *tetters* — eruptions of the skin
72 *marry* — certainly (an oath deriving from the Virgin Mary)
74 *book* — the prompt-copy of the play
76 *company* — the Children of the Chapel Royal, a boys' company (see further Commentary, p. viii)
78 *folio* — the largest size of book (referring here to full-grown actors)
78 *Jeronimo* — hero of Kyd's popular *The Spanish Tragedy* (see further Commentary, p. xxxv)
79 *decimo-sexto* — the smallest book (referring to boy actors)
82 *sooth* —truthfully
82 *needful* — necessary
82 *sallet* — salad
84 *not-received custom . . . theatre* — the outdoor Globe theatre used less extraneous music than the Blackfriars (see Commentary, p. xxiv)
88 *durst* — dare
90 *ad Parmenonis suem* — compared with the pig of Parmeno. Parmeno, famed for his ability to make pig-noises, could not compete with the real thing. Condell implies that the men will act better than the boys
91 *lost your ears* — referring to the ear-cropping of criminals
96 *baubees* — a Scottish coin of little value
96- *four of your elbows* — (i) a very shabby jacket (ii) a motley
97 fool's garment
97 *defend* — forbid
98 *censurer* — judge
99 *College of Critics* — those who practice criticism
106 *Cheap* — Cheapside, a main thoroughfare in the City of London
107 *signs* — distinguishing signs outside a house, shop, or inn (see Commentary, p. xxix)
110 *five and fifty* — ie, signs
116 *in the horse-belly* — inside the Trojan horse
120 *Hector* — Trojan hero, son of Priam and Hecuba
122 *Alexander, Achilles* — historical and legendary Greek military heroes
124 *cullion* — rascal

126   *private room* — ie, the expensive box (see note to l. 60-61,
above)
130   *extempore* — on the spur of the moment
131- *fencing of a . . . legs* — making an elaborate bow
132
135   *easy standings* — bawdy innuendo suggesting sexual positions

Dramatis Personae
4   *minion* — lover
6   *choleric* — prone to anger (though this is scarcely appropriate
to Bilioso)
17   *panderess* — female pimp, or go-between in illicit love affair
22   *halberdiers* — ceremonial guards carrying distinctive weapons,
part lance, part battleaxe

Prologus
        Staff — stanza
1   *To wrest . . . sense* — to convert each innocuous reference
into a personal accusation
3   *immodest* — unrestrained
11   *Herculean* — with the strength of the Greek hero Hercules

Act I Scene i
sd   *upper level* — the upstage balcony of the Globe Theatre
3   *Babylon* — the tower of Babel where the confusion of
tongues took place

Act I Scene ii
5   *Yaugh, god-a'-man* — an aggressive term of greeting
(untranslatable)
5   *dost* — do
5   *Ganymede* — effeminate favourite (Ganymede was Jupiter's
cupbearer of whom Juno was jealous)
9   *catamite* — young male prostitute
10   *cur* — a low-bred dog, here a surly, ill-bred fellow
11   *sullenness* — gloomy ill-temper
12   *bespurtle* — abuse, bespatter
13   *goatish-blooded* — lascivious, lustful
13   *toderers* — lustful old men
13-   *as gum into . . . fret* — inferior cloth was stiffened with gum
14   which caused it to fray. Malevole intends to irritate in a
similar way.

15   *suck up* — see what is going on
15   *Howl again* — an instruction to the musicians of the 'vilest
out-of-tune music' which starts the scene
17   *prodigious affections* — monstrous, unnatural personalities
18   *conversed with nature* — was ever born
20   *the presence* — heaven, the sight of God
23   *position* — argument, proposition
26   *affected* — disposed, inclined
26   *elements* — possibly the 'humours', the four supposed fluids
in the body thought to determine physical and mental
characteristics (phlegm, blood, choler, melancholy)
28   *halter-worthy* — deserving to be hanged
30   *palliates* — cloaks, conceals

Act I Scene iii

2   *as free as air* — no respecter of persons
4   *dissimulation* — hypocrisy
7   *usurer* — one who lends money at interest
7   *take up* — borrow
9   *a soldier's religion* — ie, one that is most profitable for him
10   *infidels* — disbelievers in religion, particularly Christianity
11   *sects* — referring to the many dissenting protestant
splinter-groups
11-   *seeming Piety . . . a petticoat* — pretended religion has
13   followed so many fashions that it's hard to know what is
truly believed
15   *a politic religion* — a religion subordinate to political
ambition
18   *doggest* — pursue, chase
20   *cozenage* — cheating, deception
21   *cuckolds* — men whose wives are unfaithful to them
26   *drabs* — strumpets, whores
26   *affected of* — desired by
27   *venery* — pursuit of sexual pleasure
28-   *Phew! the Devil . . . is everywhere* — possession by the Devil
31   was supposed to bring the gift of tongues
34   *save* — except
36   *fresh snow* — referring to the white hair of the aged Bilioso
37-   *old huddle* — miserly old fellow
38
39   *improvident* — unforseeing

40   *hugely-horned* — horns were said to grow on the foreheads of
cuckolds
40   *Duke's ox* — ie, because the Duke is cuckolding him
41   *Master Make-please* — flatterer
43-   *killing a' spiders . . . lady's monkey* — that is, performing
44   unpleasant tasks to please ladies
46   *fubbery* — cheating, deception
49   *footcloth* — a richly decorated cloth hung over a horse's back
and reaching to the ground, a sign of dignity and rank
50   *metreza* — mistress
50   *physic* — medicine
51   *pander* — a pimp, a go-between in secret love affairs
52-   *in shift of satin . . . other night* — who could wear satin one
53   day, but has hardly a shirt the next
53-   *Paris, Helen, Guinever, Lancelot* — all were adulterous lovers
55
55   *chimeras* — wild fancies
56   *conceits* — fancies, whims
56-   *Sir Tristram . . . whim-wham* — Malevole commands Prepasso
57   as if he were a performing monkey
58-   *a Knight of . . . the Huge* — Malevole mocks the knightly
62   pretensions of Prepasso
58   *trap* — a bat-and-ball game
60   *ride at the ring* — a sport in which a rider attempted to thrust
his lance through a ring
61   *fin* — eye-lid or rim
61   *welkin* — sky
62   *wild goose chase* — useless pursuit
62   *Pompey* — first century Roman general
66   *star* — fate
66   *oppress'd* — in decline, weighed down
72   *'um* — them
72   *avaunt* — begone
75   *becco cornuto* — a horned goat, ie, a cuckold
79   *tumbler* — acrobat
82   *cornutes* — cuckolds
83   *conformance* — confirmation, proof
83   *short, short!* — Tell me quickly!
85   *crone* — withered old woman
87   *sooth to say* — to tell the truth
89   *Blirt a' rhyme* — Malevole refuses to continue rhyming
90   *bawd* — procurer, brothel-keeper

90   *close* — secret
97   *hoodwinked* — blindfolded, deceived
98   *fillips* — a dismissive gesture of flicking finger and thumb,
here implying to cuckold
99   *coxcomb* — the cap worn by professional fools, shaped like a
cock's comb
99   *egregious* — prominent
102   *poniards* — daggers
106   *Catso* — obscene exclamation of disgust (from Italian 'cazzo',
penis)
108   *fairs* — fair ladies
112   *devoutful rites* — the marriage service
113   *better essence* — the soul
116   *delved-up* – dug- up
117   *tells* — counts
121   *hymenial sweets* — marital bliss
123   *court-quelquechose* — appetizer
125-   *And yet even then . . . foul knave's loins* — the implication
129   is that even when making love with her husband the
adulteress's thoughts are of her lover
129   *clips* — embraces
135   *His son* — ie, Mendoza's supposed illegitimate son, the result
of his adultery
138   *his own seed* — his own relative
140   *simony* — buying or selling religious objects or offices
141   *cope of salvation* — heaven
143   *our men* — our fellow countrymen
147   *nothing to sin with* — ie, no church property to sell
148   *shue . . . punishment* — the meaning of this passage is
uncertain
148   *intemperate* — lustful
150   *generation* — offspring
150-   *I would not . . . anything* — I would not leave my vengeance
151   to heaven (Malevole wishes to exact it himself)
151   *anything* — at all
156   *sallow* — dark, sickly yellow
157   *distemperance* — disturbance mental or physical)
164   *affected strain* — ie, the adopted speech of Malevole as a
malcontent
165   *fetterless* — unconfined, unimpeded
168   *peise my breath* — take my words seriously
169   *again* — in return

171   *a richer gem* — 'a calm heart' is more valued than a crown

Act I Scene iv
3   *Thou to whose . . . discovered* — you alone know who I truly am
6   *Ops* — wife to Saturn, goddess of plenty
9   *wanted* — lacked
10   *Suspect* — suspicion
10   *time it* — temporize, manage it
12   *bore with* — favoured
14   *suspectless* — unsuspecting
15   *lickerous* — eager for, greedy for
17   *Made strong* — allied
19   *Florentine* — ie, the Duke of Florence
24   *Citadel* — fortress commanding a city
27   *'Tis well held . . . zeal* — It is more an act of despair than enthusiasm
28   *temporize* — adapt to the time, act so as to gain time
30   *Yet* — still
31   *free-breathed discontent* — free-speaking malcontent
36   *broad-horns* — cuckolds
38   *manna* — food from heaven
39   *ranks are burst* — enemy is in disarray
39   *scuffle* — act, busy yourself
40   *durst* — dare you?
41   *mineral* — medicine
sd   *Malevole shifteth his speech* — ie, from the natural speech used to Celso to the dialect of the malcontent
44   *May-poles* — decorated high poles for dancing around (possibly referring here to the height of Sinklo the actor playing Bilioso)
45   *his breath* — his flattering speech
45   *respect in his office* — respected only for his place at Court
46   *religion in his lord* — his religion depends on that of his lord
58   *egregious* — renowned
59   *wittol* — a person content to have an unfaithful wife
59   *mummy* — decayed body
61   *disport* — entertainment
62   *chain* — an ornamental chain
66   *eat woodcocks* — a mark of wealth and sophistication, since woodcocks were expensive
66   *possetts* — hot drinks of milk curdled with wine and spiced

67   *shuttlecock* — an early form of badminton
75   *state of grace* — royal favour
78   *minions* — favourites
82   *correspondence* — amity, agreement
89   *Castilio* — an ironic reference to Castiglione, author of *The Courtier,* which defined the ideal courtier
sd   *Descries* — catches sight of
90   *privy-key* — a bawdy reference to Mendoza's carnal relations with Aurelia

Act I Scene v

sd   *Suitors* — petitioners
1   *I can and will* — ie, grant your requests
4   *God b'wi'ye!* — God be with you
6   *tripe-wife* — woman who sells tripe, a coarse woman
7   *whoreson* — detestable
7   *hot-reined* — lecherous
7   *he-marmoset* — monkey
8   *Egistus* — Aegisthus, the lover of Clytemnestra while Agamemnon led the Greeks against Troy. He was killed by Orestes
20   *Elysium* — the heaven of Greek mythology
24   *observe* — defer to, revere
24   *stateful* — dignified
26   *obsequious* — fawning, sycophantic
27   *training him* — following in his train
27   *the cloth* — covering held over a great person in a procession
27   *way proclaimed* — route cleared, procession announced
28   *vassals* — subordinates
29   *lamprels* — lampreys, an eel-like fish with seven breathing apertures on each side of the head, thought to resemble eyes
32   *brow* — face
33   *Olympus* — mountain home of the Greek gods
45   *Phaeton* — he failed to control the horses of the sun and singed the world
49   *only* — alone, for himself
50   *Phoebus* — Phoebus Apollo, god of poetry

Act I Scene vi

8   *put up* — ensure, with a clear sexual meaning as well
19   *for a spurt* — for a moment, just for sex
23   *rustiest-jawed* — foul-mouthed
24   *agin'* — against

29   *unsteadiness* — fickleness
40   *heaven's dog* — the dog star, ascendant in July and August
41   *enforcing* — ravishing
50   *fears breath* — ie, the loss of breath, death
63   *your oaths* — ie, the jewels by which Ferneze swore
65   *model* — image
73   *flashes* — outbursts
75   *election* — choice
80   *Furies* — the fearsome avenging deities of Greek mythology
84   *smock-grace* — intimate favour
84   *rail* — complain bitterly, speak abusively
88   *prevention* — anticipation, precaution
92   *forged* — fraudulent, not to be trusted
94   *given hopes* — promises
95   *blood* — passion
95   *only the* — the only

Act I Scene vii
6   *horn-mad* — enraged (because of Aurelia's unfaithfulness)
13   *centre to the glorious world* — the earth as centre of the
Ptolomaic universe
16   *tart* — sharp, biting
16   *spleenful* — irritable, passionate
17   *loose thee* — relieve you
22   *under-offices* — second-rate official duties
23   *the party* — the person
27   *closer* — more secret
27   *passages* — incidents, goings-on
28   *vows of revelation* — promises to reveal
29   *deemed* — thought, judged
32   *suspect* — suspicion
33   *save* — except
34   *reject* — rejection
35   *clipped* — embraced
36   *plain-breasted* — plain-spoken
39   *plain* — ie, unadorned with cuckold's horns
41   *phlegm* — the bodily 'humour' producing dullness of
character, evenness of temper
45   *sweet sheets* — perfumed sheets
45   *wax lights* — candles
46   *antic* — grotesquely carved
46   *cambric smocks* — delicate nightwear

46   *villainous curtains* — ie, because of the shameful deeds they conceal
47   *arras* — tapestry
47   *oiled hinges* — to silence the bedroom door
52   *deserve me* — be worthy of reward
65   *Without* — outside
69   *advanced birth* — family connection with the Medici
76   *thoughtful* — cunning
79   *brain-caught* — cunningly trapped
82   *feign* — pretend
86   *throes* — anguish, violent spasms
86   *sensible* — tangible
87-   *As bears . . . proves horrid* — as bears lick their young into an
88   adult shape men fear, so will my plans be formed

Act I Scene viii
2   *sing fool* — a punning reply. G.K. Hunter suggests perhaps 'sing full' or 'sing foul'
2   *bear the burden* — sing the refrain or the bass
3   *scurvily* — badly
4   *gelded* — castrated, emasculated
7   *good case* — good condition
8   *guarded* — expensively dressed, his clothes adorned with lace and braid
11   *fain to fool* — (i) eager to lure, (ii) keen to see
19   *growing in the woman's forehead* — in 1588 a Welsh woman was reported to have a four-inch crooked horn growing in her forehead
21   *columbine* — a drooping flower whose horned nectaries suggested cuckoldry
22   *beg fools* — ie, seek the guardianship of idiots in order to profit from their estates. Fools could be 'begged' from the King who was responsible for them
24   *begging* — stealing
30   *compliments* — accomplishments
32   *in a false gallop* — out of control
35   *Flushing* — a famous garrison-town, presumably accustomed to dubious camp followers
37   *plastic* — malleable material like wax or clay. Maquerelle can be 'worked' to procure a sexual partner
39   *smocks* — nightdresses
41   *visitant* — lover

42   *Muscovy glass* — mica, talc
43   *old lord* — ie, Bilioso
44   *conscience enough* — having no conscience
48   *Switzer* — Swiss mercenary soldier
55   *vild* — vile
59   *pettifogger* — lawyer of inferior status
59   *buckram bag* — a stiffened cloth bag traditionally used by
lawyers

Act II Scene i
sd   *a sconce* — a lantern or candlestick with a handle
sd   *the act* — the interlude music between the acts
sd   *unbraced* — with unfastened clothes
1   *woodcock* — fool (woodcocks were easily caught in snares)
3   *merely* — completely, entirely
4   *The fool . . . centaurs* — Ixion tried to ravish Juno, but
encountered only a cloud in her shape and begot the centaurs
5   *in strength of* — made strong by, confident by
6   *goat* — lecherous person
6   *goose* — fool
9   *plummets* — weights
11   *salt sallow* — salacious, excited and unhealthy
12   *thou* — ie, Ferneze
13   *suspect* — suspicion
22   *make a leg* — bow
25   *Unde cadis . . . refert* — what matters is where you fall from,
not where you fall to
26-   *What fate . . . desperate* — who can escape the revenge of a
27   desperate man?
28   *ope* — be revealed
29   *still* — always

Act II Scene ii
sd   *one door . . . other door* — the Globe Theatre is supposed to
have had two upstage doors.
1   *cast* — handful
1   *Dipsas* — a bawd in Ovid's *Amores*
1-2   *old coal* — conventional term for a pander
4   *billets* — kindling firewood
7   *lint* — kindling material
10   *Janivere* — Chaucer's *Merchant's Tale* tells of the elderly
January and his young wife May. Bilioso and Bianca conform to
these stereotypes

10   *periwinkle* — playful address to a young girl
11   *hawk* — cough
16   *maim* — injury
18   *close* — secret
18   *stock* — a thrust in fencing (*stoccado*), with a sexual meaning
18   *mortal* — able to be wounded, ie, sexually used
19   *restoratives* — aphrodisiacs
20   *Jason* — Medea helped/Jason accomplish his tasks with a
magic potion
20- *crab's guts . . . fox-stones* — alleged aphrodisiacs
22
22   *stones* — testicles
26   *country fashion* — implying it is not fashionable to be
faithful at court
27   *foregoers* — ushers, lovers
27- *whither in good deed, la, now?* — where are you really
28   going?
30- *posset with three . . . drink* — a restorative drink which has
31   three curdling processes and no liquid residue (whey)
33   *Fried frogs . . . good* — ie, good as an aphrodisiac

Act II Scene iii
9-10 *Arthur, Agamemnon, Menelaus* — all cuckolds
16   *bezzled* — befuddled, drunk
19- *Mount him aloft . . . fall* — referring to the fable of the eagle
22   who dropped the tortoise from a height to break its shell
31   *pigeon-house* — see I, iv, 85
32   *nappy fortunes* — the high and mighty ('nap' being the
rough surface of rich-textured cloths)
32   *serpigo* — a creeping skin disease
32   *strangury* — painful bladder disorder
33   *priapism* — persistent sexual erection
35   *wittolly pander* — complaisant and co-operating cuckold
36   *office* — reward, preferment
52   *corse* — corpse
53   *Tacite* — 'aside' to the audience
60   *conjure* — implore
61   *Let it be . . . may be* — ie, little known, quiet
64   *brows* — eyesight
65   *this* — ie, Ferneze's death
67   *Rivels* — wrinkles
72   *inherit* — outlive, be heir to
80   *unhele* — uncover

Act II Scene iv

1-3   *three curds . . . drink* — see note to II, ii, 30
6   *composure* — composition, recipe
7   *how does't with me?* — how does it look? how does it suit
me?
9   *Barbary hens* — Guinea fowl
13   *eringoes* — root of sea-holly, an aphrodisiac
14   *amber* — perfume
14   *Cataia* — China
15   *stones* — testicles
20   *mundifieth* — cleans
26   *honest* — virtuous, chaste
29-   *Doctor Plaster-face* — referring to the cosmetic (and so
30   remedial) quality of the drink
30-   *forging of veins* — painting life-like veins over a cosmetic
31   covering
31   *sprightening* — brightening, sparkling
32   *surfling* — painting or washing with a cosmetic
37-   *keep him not . . . pale* — don't be too cloyingly attentive to
38   your husband, lest he stray from home
42   *use* — put to use, profit from
52   *pruning, pinching and painting* — dressing-up, adorning, and
decorating
57   *sentinel* — Maquerelle, as guard to the Duchess's chamber

Act II Scene v

7   *Argus' eyes* — Argos Panoptes had eyes all over his body
22   *him* — ie, Pietro
24   *And* — if it
26   *Despite* — contempt, scorn
44   *rank* — take a stand
48   *trunk* — ie, Ferneze's body
53   *clasped* — embraced
57   *twines* — entwining
62   *spirits spent* — light and fit
63   *'scape* — escape
64   *phlegm* — see note to I, vii, 41
65   *cast a noose* — ensnared, plotted
66   *stand in honour* — defend the honour
70   *groundly* — profoundly, thoroughly
71   *provide* — make ready, prepare
72   *Prevention* — anticipation

76 *blaze* – make known, proclaim
79 *Medicis* – the notorious and powerful Florentine family
81 *Not meanly strengthful* – ie, very strong
84 *mazed* – bewildered, confused
88 *immodest waist of night* – the middle of the night (immodest because of the deeds committed at that time, and because the waist is close to the sexual organs)
89 *The mother . . . dew* – the moon
92 *inhumed* – buried
93 *kiss the pillow* – ie, sleep well
97 *name me* – adopt me (as son and heir)
100 *quit* – remove
105 *suit* – complaint, petition
112 *Huguenot* – French Protestant, meaning here 'hypocrite'
114 *fall upon* – visit
119 *Rochelle* – La Rochelle, where Huguenots found refuge from persecution
121- *King's supremacy* – the sovereign was head of the Church in
122 England
122 *things indifferent* – ie, not necessary for salvation
122- *be a Pope . . . parish* – have authority over my own
123 parishioners, tyrannize
125 *scour plough shares* – the stones of ruined churches would be left to the plough
126 *Et nunc . . . fuit* – and now corn grows where Jerusalem once stood
129 *sacredest place* – the tabernacle in the sanctuary where the Host is kept
131 *burst up* – broken open
132 *Hic finis Priami* – such was Priam's end
135 *fub* – 'cheat', a term of scornful endearment
137 *friendly Damnation* – friendly only in order to lead me to damnation
138 *descry* – observe
138 *cross-points* – dance steps, here meaning tricks, mischief
138 *courtship* – courtiership
138- *straddle as far . . . legs* – probably an allusion to the 'French
139 disease' (syphilis or the pox) which would cause such wide-legged walking
143 *Limbo* – the underworld
144 *grand cuckold, Lucifer* – like the cuckold, Lucifer has horns
148 *fame* – infamy, ill-report

152   *fly converse* — avoid relations, have nothing to do with
156   *port* — place of refuge
160   *'gins* — begins
160   *close* — secret
160   *the scene grows full* — the plot is reaching a complex climax
161   *solid skull* — sound mind

Act III Scene i

1   *waste this light* — pass the time
5   *'um* — them, ie, the hunters
6   *fain* — gladly
8   *soils* — pools or stretches of water used as a refuge by hunted
deer
23   *scriveners* — copy clerks, scribes, also a kind of moneylender
24   *Seneca* — Roman author who recommended stoic detachment
from the world while retaining a personal fortune (see further
Commentary, p. xi)
27   *died . . . coward* — Seneca cut his veins in a warm bath
35   *charges* — expenses
37   *come out* — expire
37-   *you may lay . . . for it* — ie, make your tenants suffer by
38   raising their rents
43   *saved by the teeth* — by saving on the food bill
47-   *Scotch barnacle . . . goose* — Gerard's *Herbal* (1597) refers to
48   'certain trees whereon do grow certain shells of a white
colour . . . wherein are contained little living creatures: which
shells . . . do open and out of them grow those little living things
which falling into the water do become fowls, which we call
barnacles' (ie, barnacle geese)
53   *bear their own charges* — pay for themselves
55   *watchet* — pale blue
56   *popinjay-green* — turquoise
59-   *their apparel . . . parishes* — their clothes clashing badly
60   (counties in a map were defined by different colours)
73   *good for it* — ie, good for causing gout
76   *empirics* — untrained medical practitioners
78   *Scotch boot* — an instrument of torture used in Scotland.
The leg was placed in a metal box and crushed by wedges
80   *body* — person
88   *several countrymen* — men of different countries
92   *hot-shots* — reckless hotheads
98   *Four-score . . . gentlemen* — a reference to Welsh national
pride

102 *cypress* — black crepe
102 *old* — old-fashioned
111- *salute no man . . . button* — make no low, ingratiating bows
112
130 *repine* — be discontented
130 *preferment* — advancement, promotion
134- *more melancholic . . . Prince* — because the new prince may
135 not pay off the debts of his predecessor
135 *out* — lent out
140 *the flesh . . . woodcock* — the partner (flesh) to this vision
(Madam Floria) must be a fool (woodcock)
144 *trussed and pointed* — tied and laced
145 *dog* — follow
147 *spits in my mouth* — a gesture of affection, presumably
towards an animal

Act III Scene ii

sd *frieze gown* — dressing gown
sd *patent* — letter of appointment as ambassador
2 *sober* — peaceful, subdued
5 *Unbend'st* — relaxes
9 *barb* — now
10 *wink* — sleep
12 *goodman* — a prefix to the name of persons below the rank
of gentleman
12 *tell-clock* — clock-watcher. The malcontent, being unable to
rest or sleep, can always tell the time
21 *do not put . . . bag* — keep up appearances (mutton and
porridge were second-rate fare)
26- *Hymen begins . . . robe* — Hymen, god of marriage, was
27 represented in plays and masques wearing a saffron robe.
Malevole sees a threat to Bilioso's marriage
28 *singled* — alone
29 *bordello* — brothel
34 *When* — whereas
38 *delicates* — delicacies, refined foods
40 *tricking up* — decorating, dressing-up
44 *clap* — put, place
46 *blood-full* — vigorous
47 *Ullyses absent . . . out* — the chaste Penelope resisted her
many suitors during the years of Ullyses' return from Troy by
promising to marry one when she had finished a piece of weaving.
Each night she undid the work she had finished during the day

51 *once* — one day
51 *our brows* — ie, Malevole's true face as Altofront

Act III Scene iii

6 *staggering* — fickle, unstable
6 *apace* — swiftly
7 *thorough* — through
15 *shifting* — unstable
17 *come about* — turn
19 *only force* — power alone, unique power
24 *upon their severance* — when they split apart
24 *confirm myself* — re-establish myself as Duke
28 *pair of snuffers* — instrument for cutting off the black wick from a used candle
28 *snibs* — rebukes, reproves
35 *clasp* — befriend, embrace
37 *second cause* — other reason, ulterior motive
38 *Illo, ho, ho, ho!* — cry of the falconer luring the hawk
38 *truepenny* — trusty person
43 *futuens gratis* — enjoying sex without payment
46 *sergeant* — sheriff's officer
48 *Job* — destitute and patient patriarch of the Old Testament
48 *alchemist* — an early 'scientist' who tried to transmute baser metals into gold
50 *bum-cracks* — farts
55 *gives me* — shows me, tells me
57 *stuff-clothes* — those who wear inferior, rough clothing, possibly students
58 *knocked* — had sex with
58 *sempstress* — needlewoman, seamstress
59 *pothecary* — apothecary, seller of medical drugs
60 *the Stoic* — Seneca (see note to III, i, 24, and Commentary, p. xii)
60 *Neminem servum . . . oriundum* — There is no slave who does not descend from kings, no king who does not derive from slaves
62 *touses* — pulls roughly about, dishevels
70 *grasp* — embrace
72 *get* — gain
83 *Lent and fishmongers* — fishmongers profited from Lent during which time meat-eating was forbidden
83 *cap-a-pe* — from head to foot, ie, in armour
83- *How in form?* — how is he dressed?
84

85- *who only . . . stilts* — who relies for his position on his wife's
86 powerful relatives
88 *full point* — end
96- *Lacedemonian* — whore, strumpet (Helen of Troy deserted
97 her husband Menelaus for Paris in Lacedemon, or Sparta)
105 *single him* — single him out, separate him
112 *circumstance* — narrative
114 *unpeerable* — unrivalled, unequalled
115 *honeys* — delights
116 *close to her* — deal with her, come to terms with her
122 *souls* — men
123 *virtual* — effective
123 *greatness* — ie, your promised reward

Act III Scene iv
1 *a fault* — a break in the line of scent
4 *one beast* — ie, Pietro himself, as a horned cuckold
12 *towards* — approaching
18 *My duty* — thanks
33 *sirenical* — siren-like, alluring
37 *closes* — cadences, with a sexual suggestiveness

Act III Scene v
3 *feed* — bribed
11 *Discovered* — revealed
14- *thrust his jaws awry* — put his nose out of joint
15
17 *closely* — secretly
18 *egress and regress* — free passage
19 *toused thy sheets* — rumpled your sheets, ie, slept with
your wife
23 *numbed* — silent, helpless
24- *fencing tip-tap courtiers* — those who avoid direct contact
25
29 *sleights* — trickery
32 *state* — statecraft

Act IV Scene i
8 *Cunny Court* — women's quarters (?)
11 *sentinel* — guard (see note to II, iv, 57)
18 *tongue-tied hatch* — door, with hinges oiled for silence

23   *busk-points* — corset laces, here signifying a kind of physical protection

23   *charily* — carefully

37   *defame* — infamy

38   *note* — observation

41   *dares* — defies

41   *quite* — clear

44   *presently* — immediately

47   *servant* — probably lover (see line 50 below)

56   *draw Ullyses' bow* — a legendary mark of strength (Penelope demanded this of her suitors)

61   *fortune of his beard* — his fortune as an adult

Act IV Scene ii

sd   *a measure* — a stately dance

2-3   *Les quanto . . . brawl* — names of dances

6-10   *two singles on . . . doubles* — steps and movements involved in the dance 'Bianca's Brawl'

11   *honour* — curtsy

12   *Daedalus* — he constructed a maze for Minos of Crete

25   *burying* — covering

Act IV Scene iii

17   *cold sweat of night* — dew

20   *heady Neptune* — violent waves

21   *eased my limbs* — sat down

34   *extinct* — extinguished

36   *minioning* — caressing

38   *blood* — passion

38   *slave* — enslave

39   *washed an Ethiop* — attempted to redeem a sinner (by marrying her). (G.K. Hunter quotes Tilley's *Dictionary of Proverbs*)

41   *black* — sullied, defiled

44   *dull* — listless, unresponsive

46   *souse* — plunge

49   *nicer-stomached* — discriminating, delicate

56   *hearty* — heartfelt

60   *over-jump* — pass over

63   *on death* — on pain of death

69   *address to* — prepare for

71   *wit* — intellect, intelligence

72   *presence* — public appearance
73   *politician* — a schemer
77   *slatted* — dashed, smashed
82   *kennel* — gutter
83   *brain-pan* — head
86-   *praemium incertum . . . scelus* — uncertain is the reward he
87   seeks, certain is the crime
87   *How stands the progress?* — how are your plans
progressing?
91   *circumstance* — detail
98   *Elder* — a senior member of the Presbyterian church
100   *inward* — intimate
103- *broad a' speaks* — coarsely, freely he speaks
104
105   *go for* — walk because of
109   *consort* — accompany
111   *laid* — blamed
112   *Scud* — make haste
114   *buff-captain* — leather-jerkined soldier
115   *Westphalian gammon-faced* — pig-faced (Westphalia was
famous for bacon)
115   *zaza* — bully?
117   *Castle of Comfort* — the citadel where Maria is held
118   *sha't!* — You shall!
125   *Thou'st* — you must
129   *stalking-horse* — horse trained to allow a hunter to conceal
himself behind it
134   *opposite* — opponent
135   *sad suspect* — heavy suspicion
140   *Imbraids* — upbraids, reproaches
140   *beholdingness* — indebtedness
141   *like deed, not doer* — we approve the crime but not the
criminal

Act IV Scene iv
3   *unclasp itself* — release its fury
4   *rand* — rant
6   *infidel* — unbeliever
13   *Cross capers* — dancing steps
14   *eldern guns* — popguns made of elderwood
18   *brokers* — pawnbrokers
30   *perfect* — certain

Act IV Scene v

sd   *halberts* — halberdiers (ceremonial guards)
sd   *base* — befitting an inferior person
9   *yet* — even though
10   *sad* — heavy
13   *tilts* — a combat sport between two horsemen armed with lances
13   *tourneys* — tournaments
16   *battery* — assault
17   *usherless* — without ceremony, unannounced
18   *rheumy vault* — damp cave
28   *joy triumph* — enjoy your triumph
33   *part* — leave
36   *Brake* — broke
38   *reprobate* — sinner
45   *brackish* — lascivious
47   *impudence* — shamelessness
48   *sap* — juice, fluid
57   *twelve kings' beards* — the legendary King Arthur defeated the Saxon kings in twelve battles
59   *got forty . . . night* — referring to the fifty daughters of Thespius
64   *tent* — probe and clean a wound
65   *ground* — limit
71   *coal basket* — carrying coals (a servile task)
71   *common usher . . . place* — ie, it is chance rather than merit that raises people socially
87   *Yet* — at the moment
89   *turn straight again* — return immediately
91   *run still* — stay with, go along with
100   *Amphitryo* — Alcmena's husband
105   *flesh-fly* — parasite
105- *lean galled backs* — the poorest people
106
110   *Golgotha* — graveyard
111   *draught* — cesspool, privy
113   *orbs* — stars
117   *pair of shears* — scissors that cut the 'one piece' (l. 116) of cloth
118   *glossing* — finishing
121   *confounds* — destroys, overthrows
122   *regency* — royalty

124 *sleight* — trick
127 *dread power* — God
145 *touseth* — pulls roughly about
145 *maze* — amazement
147 *close can temporize* — secretly and effectively bides his time
148 *detect* — expose, reveal
149 *lest ignorance fear suspect* — in case the ignorant think I am afraid to do so
150 *close* — meet

Act V Scene i

4   *Monsieur Gundi* — Jeromo de Gondi was French Ambassador to London in 1578
5   *platter* — plate
7-8   *be coistered* — the word is unknown: possibly 'suffer agonies'
16   *pomander* — a perfumed ball
17,   *musk, civet* — sweet-smelling substances
18
20   *aqua-vitae* — water of life (meaning a restorative spirit such as brandy)
33   *stinkards* — mob
34   *carted* — ie, carted through the streets (a punishment for sexual offenders)
38   *pate* — head
50   *answer a man* — respond to a challenge to a duel
54   *anon* — immediately
55   *presence* — royal presence-chamber

Act V Scene ii

3   *usquebaugh* — whisky
4   *the (   )* — obviously 'pox'
11   *pestered* — overcrowded
20   *the City* — the business centre of London, home of money-lenders
21   *take up* — borrow
21   *forbearance* — credit
24   *I'll take it so* — I'll drink that toast
35   *Griffon* — a hero in Ariosto's *Orlando Furioso*
35   *quean* — bawd
40   *transformation of state* — ie, the rise of Mendoza
46   *officers* — officers of the law, sergeants
60   *sign* — astrological sign of the zodiac

62   *moment* — importance, weight
63   *Chaldean* — astrologer, soothsayer
67-   *Pisces, Cancer, Capricorn, Libra, Scorpio* — astrological signs
71   of the Fish, Crab, Goat, Scales, Scorpion
68   *precisian's* — puritan's (one who is rigidly strict in religious
and moral matters)
71   *at the term* — (i) at the court of law, (ii) impotent
81   *buff-jerkin* — soldier's clothing
82   *attend* — await
88   *carriage* — behaviour
90   *fine* — fee

Act V Scene iii

3   *tender* — offer
15   *Mully* — familiar form of Mary, a term of endearment
17-   *in despite of . . . Phoebo* — ie, more splendidly than these
18   heroes of the chivalric romance *The Mirror of Knighthood*
32   *Cleopatra's asps, Portia's coals* — Cleopatra killed herself by
snake bites, Portia by swallowing hot coals: both resisted
'enforcement'
39   *cockatrice* — whore
40   *his feather* — compare note to Induction, 40-2
42   *hunt the letter* — find a suitable alliteration (for 'sex')
44-   *stultorum plena . . . omnia* — fools are everywhere
45
46   *sleights* — cunning, trickery
49   *niceness* — coyness
51   *put her to't* — persuade her
51   *flax* — inflammable material
57   *spleeny* — ill-tempered, irritable
61   *lime-twig* — snare (for Maria). Branches were smeared with
lime to catch birds
75-   *Si quoties . . . homines* — if as often as men sin . . . (Bilioso
76   leaves the quotation incomplete. 'There is no point in
punishing every single sin' is its general sense)
78   *collogue* — speak deceitfully
80   *nemo omnibus . . . sapit* — the translation follows: no man
can be honest at all hours
85   *purchase* — acquire titles
95   *and* — if

Act V Scene iv

10 *returns* — replies
13 *resolute* — resolved
15 *Per scelera . . . iter* — the safest way through crimes is always by crimes
18 *undersheriff* — law officer who arrested men on behalf of the sheriff
20 *scrivener* — see note to III, i, 23
23 *bastinado* — a punishment involving beating on the soles of the feet
28- *tails off* — turns tail
29
33- *your whore went . . . puritan* — see Commentary, p. xxxviii
34
39 *conduits* — nostrils
49 *fame* — infamy
56 *observe ye* — obey
59 *instalment* — coronation
68 *Mercury* — as guide of the dead
68 *gratulate* — welcome
70 *far-fet* — far-fetched
73 *graced* — accepted, welcomed
73 *take* — hold the audience, captivate
75 *close* — ungenerous
78 *wreaths* — the crown
80 *out of deserved ranks* — simply because he has a proper bodyguard
83 *senseless* — indifferent
91- *Great Leader* — God
92

Act V Scene v

2-3 *great chamber* — assembly room at court
3-4 *drop your torch* — spill the pitch from your torch
9 *scaffolds* -- raised platforms for spectators
10 *enow* — enough
14 *stale cut* — out of fashion
15 *felt and feather* — a felt hat with a feather in it
16 *tiring things* -- head-dresses
18 *falling-bands* — fashionable turned-down collars (now replacing the ruff)
22 *poting-stick* — used for adjusting and setting pleats

24   *Signior . . . Jaques* — referring to a type of Scottish courtier who followed James I to London in 1603 seeking favour
28   *Marshall Make-room* — an usher
28-   *in reversion* — the next in line to the position
29
35-   *as fine a man . . . legs* — supposedly a reference to Marston
36   himself
38   *Quidlibet in Quodlibet* — whichever in whatever (possibly a legal pun, whose sense is now uncertain)

Act V Scene vi
2   *o'er-peise* — outweigh
2   *slight rites* — mere ceremonies (ie, Maria's marriage)
17   *scant of* — deficient in
23   *You'st* — you must
27   *innated* — innate
30   *urge* — intensify
42   *girt* — bind
56   *Cyllenian* — Mercury was born on Mount Cyllene
57   *lower coasts* — lower regions, Hades
62   *depending* — awaiting settlement, pending
65   *Mercury shall . . . lawyer* — Mercury is patron of lawyers
73   *apt to* — fitted for, given to
sd   *one change* — a change of partners in the dance
95-   *cony-catching* — cheating, deceiving
96
102-   *sixpenny damnations* — common prostitutes
103
104   *pole-cats* — prostitutes
108   *receive* — understand
sd   *bending* — aiming
127   *impudent* — shameless
132   *achieve thee* — kill you
147   *still conceit* — always remember
152   *spited at* — treated spitefully
152-   *like apricocks* — apricots were left to ripen against south-
153   facing walls
158   *put it up* — put up with it
161   *suburbs* — brothels were situated in the suburbs
165   *idle* — unoccupied

Epilogus

1   *heedy* — attentive
2   *illness* — flaw
3   *merely* — utterly
8   *breaks* — errors, flaws
9   *detect* — expose
13   *another's* — Ben Jonson's (the play is dedicated to Jonson)
14   *Thalia* — the comic Muse
15   *lamps* — insights

Above: Malevole taunts the usurping Duke Pietro as a cuckold
(Act 1, Scene 3). *Below:* Maquerelle acts as go-between for
Aurelia and Ferneze (Act 1, Scene 6)

Above: Malevole banters with the ambitious courtier Mendoza
(Act 1, Scene 5). *Below:* Malevole with the bawd Maquerelle
(Act 2, Scene 2)

Above: From left to right, Count Equato, the fool Passarello, Mendoza, Bilioso and the departing Duke Pietro (Act 3, Scene 1).
Below: Maquerelle relates the events of the previous night to the Duchess's ladies (Act 4, Scene 1).

Above: Malevole pretends to Mendoza that the 'hermit' is safely poisoned (Act 5, Scene 4). *Below:* Mendoza begs the masquers for mercy at the end of the play (Act 5, Scene 6)